W9-ARM-179

Consultative Selling

Third Edition

Mack Hanan

American Management Association

This book is available at a special discount when ordered in bulk quantities. For information, contact Special Sales Department, AMACOM, a division of American Management Association, 135 West 50th Street, New York, NY 10020.

Library of Congress Cataloging-in-Publication Data

Hanan, Mack.
Consultative selling.

Includes index.
1. Selling. 2. Selling—Key accounts. I. Title.
HF5438.25.H345 1985 658.8'1 85-47677
ISBN 0-8144-5832-7

Printing number

10 9 8 7 6 5 4 3 2

Three Tests of a Successful Sales Strategy

If you have a me-too commodity product that you cannot differentiate and you sell it in a mature market under fierce price competition, can you improve its profits without changing the product?

If you have a new product with a true technological difference that gives you unique performance benefits, can you maintain its initial high margins without changing the product, even after the entry of lower-priced competitors who offer equal or greater advantages?

If you have a technologically inferior product, can you improve its profits without changing the product?

One sales strategy, Consultative Selling, has been passing these three tests since 1970. Me-too commodity products are being sold at high margins long past their point of maturity. New products are maintaining their initial margins long after they have been replicated or surpassed by competition. Inferior products are having their margins reborn, their market share restored, and their former leadership positions regained, all without spending a dollar on product renovation.

No other sales strategy can make these statements.

To my partners, ***Jim Cribbin, Jack Donis,*** and ***Herman Heiser,*** who set out with me to improve the profits of our clients and who, along the way, enriched me with their knowledge, their skills in implementing it, and their discipline in hanging in with me until each new level of innovation became familiar.

Contents

The Consultative Selling Mission: Why Should You Sell Like a Consultant? **1**

Part I *Consultative Positioning Strategies*

1 How to Become Consultative **17**
2 How to Penetrate High Levels **36**
3 How to Merit High Margins **45**

Part II *Consultative Proposing Strategies*

4 How to Qualify Customer Problems **63**
5 How to Quantify Your Solution **82**
6 How to Sell the Customer's Return **102**

Part III *Consultative Partnering Strategies*

7 How to Set Partnerable Objectives **121**
8 How to Agree on Partnerable Strategies **128**
9 How to Ensure Partnerable Rewards **147**

Appendixes

A Rebranding Strategy for Consultative Selling of Mature Products **158**

B Marketcentering Strategy for Consultative Selling to Dedicated Markets **162**

C Financial Strategy for Consultative Selling of Capital-Intensive Systems **169**

Index **196**

The Consultative Selling Mission: Why Should You Sell Like a Consultant?

Consultative Selling is profit improvement selling. It is selling to high-level customer decisionmakers who are concerned with profit—indeed, who are responsible for it, measured by it, evaluated by it, and accountable for it. Consultative Selling is selling at high margins so that the profits you improve can be shared with you. High margins to high-level decisionmakers: this is the essence of Consultative Selling.

Since 1970, Consultative Selling has revolutionized key account sales. It has helped customer businesses grow, and supplier businesses achieve new earnings along with them. Everywhere it is practiced, Consultative Selling replaces the traditional adversary buyer-seller relationship with a win-win partnership in profit improvement. This is no mean feat. To accomplish it, Consultative Selling requires strategies that are totally divorced from vendor selling. It means that you stop selling products and services and start selling the impact they can make on customer businesses. Since this impact is primarily financial, selling consultatively means selling new profit dollars—not enhanced performance benefits or interactive systems, but the new profits they can add to each customer's bottom line.

Consultative Selling is selling a dollar advantage, not a product or process advantage. There is no way to compromise this mission. Anything less is vending.

Consultative Selling versus Vending

Vendors sell price-performance benefits to purchasing agents. Consultative sales representatives sell up. They form partnerships with business function managers whose processes they improve. They also partner with line-of-business managers whose sales they improve. These are their first levels of partnership. They also partner at the purchasing level, forming a relationship that permits both partners to work with function managers and line managers in a triad of mutual interests. This is the consultative uniqueness. No vendor using allegedly "professional selling skills" can replicate it.

Vendors have many adversaries, both customers and competitors. Consultative sellers have just one partner. This relationship is bedrock. "Your unique Consultative Selling has helped me earn the President's Award twice," a consultative sales representative has said. "This is an unprecedented achievement in the history of my company. To quantify that, it represents thousands of bonus dollars plus a European vacation for two. I know I should take my wife. But my customer partner deserves it more."

Vendors bid in a crowd, reacting to requests for proposal. Consultative sellers takes the initiative and seek out profit opportunities for their customers. When they propose, there are no competitors.

Vendors use their product catalogs as their sales database. Consultative sellers use databases of facts and figures about their customers' operations as their source of knowledge about what to sell, and how, and to whom.

Vendors are only as good as their last price. Consultative sellers are as good as their last improvement in customer profit and the continuity they have built into it so that the next opportunity, and the next, are implicit to the customer.

Vendors spend their sales life trying to be accepted as an alternative supplier of products. Consultative sellers gain acceptance as exclusive partners in creating new profits. Vendors can be terminated by a small difference in price. To dislodge a consultant requires proof of a significant difference in profits and a deteriorated partnership.

For these reasons, no vendor can compete with a properly trained consultative sales representative. Even retrained vendors cannot stay in the game if they have been given only the cosmetics of consultative positioning without a solid foundation in the economics of customer operations and the financial savvy to make a positive change in them.

Cosmetized vendors have their powdered wigs blown off when they try to pass as consultants—not by their competitors but by their customers. It may take the customer a while after a sale to find out whether a vendor's product works. But the customer knows even *before* the sale whether a consultant's proposed profit is really going to be forthcoming and whether its proposal is based on accurate knowledge or guesswork.

Professing to be able to touch a customer's bottom line means that there is no place to hide up front. Unfortunately, by the time an ill-trained vendor's disguise has been revealed, those who ill-trained him or her have already collected on the sale of their bill of goods. Like the Music Man, they have gone elsewhere.

The 80–20 Rule of Sales Management

From the inception of Consultative Selling in 1970, it has become the sole successful strategy for selling major products, equipment, systems, or services at high margins to major customers. All other products sold to all other customers should be vended, because the return from selling them in a consultative manner cannot repay the investment.

This is simply an application of the Pareto Principle, the 80–20 rule. The 20 percent of all sales that carry 80 percent of the high-margin unit profits should come regularly from Consultative Selling. The remaining 80 percent of sales, which yield low unit profits, should continue to come from vending. Sometimes the same sales representative does both. But more and more, Consultative Selling is a specialty. Every minute that a skilled consultative seller spends vending means an unaffordable loss of premium profits on both sides—supplier and customer.

This means that the heyday of monolithic selling is over. Price-performance selling should be confined to the purchasing level. This is the level that issues requests for proposals and invites bids whose sole significant deviation from each other will most likely be in price. If you have mature products, services, or systems whose performance is more or less replicated by competition, they should be vended as commodities in the least costly manner.

To be unusually profitable, you must concentrate on the top tier, for that is where the profits are. In most cases, they are underexploited. It is safe to say that whatever your current profits from key account sales, they are probably one-third to two-thirds less than their potential. If this estimate seems high, reduce it by half; if it still seems high, halve it further. It is still a formidable opportunity, the equivalent of developing a new growth market. Yet it offers far fewer risks than a new market and far more cost-effective rewards.

The risk-reward ratio of key account selling is so unusually favorable because of one unique attribute. A key account is defined as a customer whose profits you can improve significantly, improving your own profits significantly at the same time. As a result, key account customers *want* you to sell to them whenever you can demonstrate your ability to improve their profits. If you do not fully capitalize on your sales opportunity, you deprive your customers of added profits. In Consultative Selling, customer sales insistence takes the place of sales resistance.

No less risky strategy for profit growth exists than key account concentration. No greater opportunity to profit from sales exists than maximizing top tier penetration. And there is no business growth strategy more certain or more capable of quick and consistent payoff.

Knowing the Customer's Business

The top tier, where key account selling must take place, is concerned with policy: where to allocate funds to solve priority problems and seize priority opportunities. At the business function management level, the concern is for strategies to achieve these priorities. As a result, the top tier shuns traditional vendor tactics. It is unresponsive to feature and benefit comparisons. It stares glassy-eyed at laundry lists of ingredients, components, formulas, subsystems, process variations, or more inclusive warranties. It ignores price as a reason to buy, resists the bait of a trial close, and does not take kindly to having its objections overcome. From its perspective, so-called professional selling is amateurish selling. The top tier deals with vendors simply by declining to deal with them.

Companies that do not respect two-tier selling always ask how they can "sell up." "How can we get our sales representatives to stand before a top-level decisionmaker?" They ask the wrong question. Any vendor can make it to the top once. The right question is, "How can we get our representatives invited back a second time?" Unless that happens, no new knowledge of the customer's business—and consequently no decision to buy—will flow to them.

How can key account representatives be invited back? There is only one way. On their first call, they must present new knowledge of the customer's business—not knowledge of their own business, not product or process knowledge, not knowledge of their latest terms, conditions, or deals, but knowledge of the customer's business and ways to improve it. This is the crucial difference between top tier and bottom tier selling. The bottom tier wants to hear about the seller's business; the top tier wants only to learn more about its own.

Concentrating on key account penetration inescapably means concentrating on knowing the businesses of your key accounts. It means knowing customer problems and the dollar values of those problems. It means knowing customer opportunities and the dollar values of those opportunities. It means knowing how you can help solve the problems and help achieve the opportunities. It means knowing the dollar values of your solutions. It means bringing this information into your business in the form of a key account database and positioning the database as the foundation of your key account penetration.

Operating as a Financial Service Business

The decision to concentrate on key account selling as the bull's-eye of sales management is, first of all, a decision to manage from a base of customer data, not products. It puts you in the information business. It acknowledges your recognition of the central fact about top tier selling: For both seller and buyer, information makes up 90 percent of every transaction. Nothing moves until the information moves.

Knowledge of how to improve their businesses is the principal element in any sale to key account customers. It possesses reality because it is their business. Nothing, including your physical hardware, is as real for them as that. When you talk about your products, you may think you are discussing tangibles if they have weight, size, shape, texture, color, or aroma. But these are simple bits and pieces of information. They become significant only when you can connect them to the reality of a customer's business by showing the financial values they will deliver. In Consultative Selling, *only financial values,* not products, are tangible.

Marketing Financial Values

When you decide to concentrate on the penetration of your top tier business opportunity, you must give up the traditional positioning of your business. If you currently define the nature of your business in product terms, or in terms of its raw materials or its processes, you will remain a vendor. So it will be with any definition that has to do with your own business instead of your relationship to the business of your key accounts. From the customer's perspective, which must now become your own, your business is a financial service business whose "product" is improved customer profit.

Financial service businesses are information businesses; they deal with information about monetary values. They act as stewards of their customers' financial well-being, and consult on the most cost-effective strategies for appreciating each customer's current worth. They are evaluated by results that appear in black and white on the customer's bottom line. Were profits improved? Were they improved as much as promised? Could they have been improved even more? Could they have been improved even faster? Will they continue to be improved? Can someone else improve them more?

How consultative is each key account representative? Their report cards are contained in their customers' answers to these questions. But what about the age-old question: Can they sell? Unless the other questions can be answered positively by their customers, selling—in the vendor mode of price-performance comparisons—may be the worst thing that top tier sales representatives can do.

Key account representatives must position themselves as financial service representatives. This does not mean they *sell* a financial service; it means they *provide* a service that delivers improved profitability for their customers. They sell the profit. If your business has a strong product heritage, it may be initially difficult for you to reposition your offerings from hardware to hard dollars; from something that goes into a customer's business to something that comes out of its improved operation; from something that is a commodity to something that is uniquely branded.

If you are in the electronic data processing business, you will have to learn how to sell the improved profits resulting from solving a customer's problems through data processing rather than selling an EDP system itself.

If your company manufactures materials cleaning machinery, you will have to learn how to sell the improved profits resulting from solving a customer's cleaning problems rather than selling cleaning equipment itself.

If your company processes food, you will have to learn how to sell the improved retail profits resulting from stocking your products rather than selling the products themselves.

A financial service business lives or dies on its ability to create measurable and attributable gains on a customer's bottom line. The gains must be presented in dollar terms, the customer must be able to attribute them to you, and you must be able to do it again. The customer's added profit is your "product." There is no way to hide it if it is significant, and there is no way to hide from it if it is not.

Planning Individual Account Penetration

Concentrating on top tier penetration requires planning. You must penetrate every key account to its maximum contribution. You must penetrate as quickly as possible because time is money, both for you and for your customers. You must penetrate at high levels to ensure top tier representation. You must penetrate on a consecutive sequential basis so you will always be at work improving a key account's profits and avoiding downtime in applying your consultative skills.

You must penetrate in such a way that you can upgrade your penetrations over time and migrate into new opportunities. You must penetrate the most significant customer problems on a priority timetable. In this way, the customer's most compelling needs are benefited first, and you will be able to close off invasion routes from competitors who will be attracted to gaps you leave unfilled. You must accomplish these tasks with every key customer account because each is a miniature market of its own—a microcosm of an industry to which you are committed because you can help it improve its profits and it can help you improve your own.

Each account penetration plan is a blueprint of how the profit contribution of a customer will be maximized. It is objective-oriented. Its strategies are composed of the proposals that form the "product line" that you will deliver to the account this year. It tells you how important you are to each customer.

In turn, the improved profit that will accrue to you is the customer's contribution. It tells how important the customer is to you, how "key" its key account status really is. If your contribution to the customer turns out not to be significant, you will lose your position as a consultant. If the customer's contribution to you is not significant and cannot be made so, you should by the same token demote the customer to a vendor relationship.

Partnering in Profit

There is only one platform from which you can operate when your objective is to manage key account penetration for improved profit on sales: that is to recognize the primacy of improved profit within your key account businesses and make it your Number 1 objective. Of all the dependencies on which key account penetration rests, first and foremost is to create with each customer a partnership for improved profitmaking.

Partnering in mutual profit improvement is the basis for win-win relationships. It requires a dedication to do your homework, to get the facts and quantify their implications in dollar terms. It requires a dedication to install solutions rather than merely sell them—to put them in place, monitor their contribution, and teach your customer partners how to maintain the profit-improving rate you have proposed.

Partnering is an endless cycle where homework leads to a proposal, which leads to a sale, which leads to upgrading the sale and developing new information about the customer's business, which serves as homework for the next proposal, and so on, endlessly.

Partnering takes place at every stage of the consultative process, because every stage involves the customer's people. The two most productive stages are the discovery of problems that can be solved together, and the achievement of their solutions. This tells you the secret of consultative partnerships. They are based on two kinds of rewards. One is *shared learning:* finding out how to solve a problem that is inhibiting a customer's profits. The other is *shared profitmaking:* proving that your partnership works by delivering tangible dollar results.

Bringing the Customer In

The traditional vendor concept of a penetration system suggests a one-way objective, getting into customer businesses. In consulting, penetrating works both ways. While you are broadening and deepening your presence inside customer businesses, the customer knowledge that is being gained is flowing back to you. The customer is being brought in.

Nothing more salubrious can happen to the sales function. The customer has always been its missing link. Historically, it has contained product knowledge, process knowledge, pricing knowledge, and promotional knowledge in profusion. These are all internal areas of information that have dramatized the "me-ness" of most sales functions. Rarely have they been sufficiently customer-oriented to the "they" out there. The closest to knowing about what goes on "out there" has been competitive knowledge. But even this has been focused on competitive products, processes, pricing, and promotion.

A key account penetration database internalizes customers. It brings them inside your business in the form of data about their most significant problems and opportunities that you can affect.

Bringing customers into your business means knowing their cost problems, the values they assign to their opportunities, and their objectives. Their objectives are their targets, and they will try to reach them by two types of strategies: solving their cost problems, and expanding their sales opportunities. Consultative Selling allows you to help them do both. But you will be unable to help them until you know what they know.

To bring in your customers means never having to say you don't know.

When customers are inside your decisionmaking system, you will be unable to ignore them at the all-important initial stages of proposal, where all sales are really made. The presence of customer knowledge will affect not only your proposals but how you go about making them. "Get the customer in here"—in the form of customer data—will become your most insistent demand. Without it, you will be embarrassed at your nakedness.

Customers, no longer strangers, outsiders, or adversaries, will become familiar. You will get the feel of their businesses. Their problems and opportunities will be your starting points for selling, not your products. All the usual vendor sales points—how the products are made, how they perform, and what their price may be—will become subservient to what you know about your customers. If sales features have value, it will be in relation to adding operating and financial value to your customers. If there is no value they can add, there is no value they can claim.

Diffusing Traditional Buyer-Seller Roles

When customers have been brought into your business as residents in your sales database and when you have penetrated their businesses in depth, breadth, and height, the traditional distinctions between buyer and seller will become diffused. Their basis, which lies in the absence of mutual objectives, will have disappeared. Win-lose sales strategies will have no place. Because your customers must win if you are going to have a growing market, and because you must win if your customers are going to have a growing improvement in their profits, your combined need for win-win relations will foster a new union in your roles.

The line between selling and buying will gray out. The zone where customer interests conflict with your interests will thin down. Your need to overcome them will be converted to a need to come over to their way of assigning priorities to their problems, defining the kinds of solutions they can most readily accept, and together with them, implementing the solutions inside their businesses.

You will still have to compete to serve them. But once accepted, you will become their partners in profit. Your common objectives will be identified in your penetration plans; both of you will have signed off on them. The strategies will be known to both of you and approved by your customers so that they can work together with you to achieve shared objectives.

In such a scenario, which is commonplace in Consultative Selling relationships, who is buyer and who is seller—and what difference does it make? Your role will be that of a customer extender, acting as an extension of your customer's own people and their capabilities to solve their problems. Thus you can become positioned as a true adder of value. Your contribution is perceptible; it is also quantifiable.

The essence of role blending is your combined ability to achieve the dollar objectives of your account penetration plan. This is your pivot point in moving away from vending toward consultation. If you fail, you fall back to being a vendor. You separate out of the partnership and become a supplier once again, perceived as having your own self-serving objectives that are bound to be inconsistent with—indeed, they are adversarial to—the needs of your customers.

Optimizing Key Account Contribution

The fact that a customer is a key account does not mean that all your transactions will automatically be the big-winner type that yields both of you major amounts of profits. The 80–20 rule mandates that 80 percent of all transactions produce only 20 percent of profit contribution, either to you or to customers. It is the remaining 20 percent of sales that makes the key account relationship so productive of growth profits. It produces 80 percent of mutual profits.

The single most critical element in managing a key account sales force is providing a systematic method for concentrating time and talent on the most productive proposals.

What composes the 80 percent, and what composes the 20 percent?

The bulk of key account transactions—80 percent—generally consists of proposing more or less repetitive solutions to standard, recurrent problems: improving profit by advancing the collection of receivables, or by decreasing inventory carrying costs, or by increasing productivity of a business function, or by stepping up sales. These problems may prevail throughout a key account's operating divisions, or they may be epidemic only in a single division. Sometimes every account in the same industry will have identical problems, because they come with the industry. To deal with them most cost-effectively, standardized solutions can be proposed, installed, and monitored in a virtually standardized manner.

Using standardized solutions to standard, recurrent problems will release selling time and talent for the smaller category of key account sales, the 20 percent.

Two types of situations constitute this 20 percent category. One is made up of semistandardized solutions to standard problems; they have a one-time uniqueness about them that makes a standardized solution unworkable. The second situation is the custom-tailored solution. This represents the apex of your ability to solve what is usually an exceptional, or a once-in-a-long-time, problem of major importance to a customer's business. The custom-tailored solution must be your highest-ticket item because it reflects the highest value that you can confer on a customer.

Custom-tailored solutions can provide multiple profit opportunities. Initially, they yield premium profits based on their premium value for the original customer. Next, they can generate additional premium profits by adaptation to closely similar problems, either with the same customer or with others in the same industry. Finally, some of them can eventually become semistandardized or standardized solutions for sale to several key accounts.

The more you focus on selling customized solutions, the greater opportunity you will have to maximize your contribution to key customers as well as the contribution you receive from them. This is the classic challenge of being a consultative seller or managing a consultative sales force.

Answers to Questions Sales Representatives Ask

"How do we know we can become consultative sellers?" Sales representatives often ask this question as they try to match their own perceived abilities with the strategies of the consultative approach. "How can we tell that we have what it takes?" The only way to know for certain, of course, is to apply consultative strategies to a key account. But even beforehand, sales representatives can preview themselves in a relatively straightforward manner by evaluating three aspects of their talent mix.

Motivation comes first. Do you have the desire to develop professional knowledge about a customer's business, especially its manufacturing and marketing processes? *Dedication* is a second consideration. Do you have the dedication necessary to explore a wide range of optional ways to improve the customer's profit, knowing in advance that you will have to reject or rework most of them before you can hope to install them, and that even then you will have to monitor and measure their progress long after the excitement of their novelty has worn off? The third essential talent is the ability to achieve your own *self-actualization* largely through contributing to the enrichment of your customers.

Sales representatives also want to know how their key accounts are likely to react to them when they make their opening consultative approach. "Will we have to motivate a customer to accept us in our new role? How do we get started: Do we suddenly announce that from now on we are going to be consultative salesmen?" When you try for the first time to position yourself consultatively with a key account, you may encounter reactions ranging from polite curiosity to skepticism. You will have to change your image with care and credibility. A good way to face the problem is to introduce the change something like this:

"Up to this point, my contribution to our relationship has been based on assuring you of a supply of products and product-related services that have been helpful to you in earning a greater profit from your operations or on the sales you make to your customers. Now I want to begin to emphasize my ability to improve your profit in a more systematic manner."

The response you seek is the question, "What is your plan?" You can then reply, "My plan is to help reduce the cost of one of your major operations by X dollars or Y percent." Or "I propose to help you improve the profit from sales of one of your major products by X dollars or Y percent."

When the customer asks the magic question, "How?" you can begin the consultative sell.

Because Consultative Selling obviously requires a serious time commitment to a customer's business, sales representatives want to know how to reconcile it with results. "Suppose we get ourselves deeply involved? What happens if we lose the account? How do we justify our investment?'' By getting involved in a customer's business through adding profit to it, a seller is taking the single most effective step toward consolidating a long-term lasting relationship. Profit improvement is the best insurance policy against all but capricious account losses or those that occur for reasons removed from the seller's interaction with the customer. By definition, key accounts are too valuable to lose. For this reason they are worth serving with the strategy that can help them the most and bind them the closest to their most helpful source of supply.

In selling, sauce for the goose soon becomes sauce for the gander. However unique it may be, no product and no sales strategy remains exempt from competitive imitation for very long. ''Is this not also true of Consultative Selling?'' sales representatives often ask. ''What happens when everybody is selling consultatively? Haven't we just escalated competition to a higher level of cost and complexity?'' Since Consultative Selling is the standard for all key account relationships, there is no doubt that each supplier will have to match competition by adopting it. The greatest rewards will go to the company that adopts it first.

But even if all suppliers copy each other's Consultative Selling strategy and even if each offers to improve profit for customers, Consultative Selling does not permit exact replication. This is because *it is a service and not a product*. Only products can be standardized. Services can always remain ''branded''—that is, made unique, because of the personal nature of their application. All suppliers in an industry may offer Consultative Selling. Each customer will prefer to deal with only one of them, however, because of the particular human and operating values created by an individual sales representative who is skilled in applying personal capabilities to the customer's business. In the final analysis, the branded added value offered by selling consultatively is the personal service of the seller.

Summing Up the Consultative Selling Mission

Bringing the customer into your key account planning will radically change your sales performance. Once the customer is in, you can justly describe your operations as being customer-driven and market-oriented. Once in, you can begin to build customer acceptance from the very start of the proposal process instead of only hoping to obtain it at the end. Once in, the connection between customer profits and your own profits will become bonded. Neither of you will ever let the other forget it.

If you accept these implications of managing major customer sales, then you will be able to take command of Consultative Selling's fundamental task: maximizing the value of your most perishable resource, the time that key customer representatives spend with top tier decisionmakers. This is "time on target," the most critical and elusive element in selling. Because it is dispensed at the pleasure of your key account customers, it cannot be bought, cajoled, or consistently manipulated. It can only be earned.

The entry and reentry price for penetrating to the top tier is the same. You must bring new output from your database. You must also bring new achievement. This is the core of your proposals. These two components of the partnering process—new learning about customer problems and new profits from solving them—are the products of Consultative Selling.

"For the first time," key account representatives have said, "I feel that my customers are really listening to me. And why not? It's their businesses I'm talking about, not mine. They really want me to sell, because they want the improved profits they know I can bring. As a result, it's no longer clear to me whose job I'm doing, theirs or mine. It's no longer clear to them, either. Maybe that's why we're working so well together."

Consultative Positioning Strategies

1

How to Become Consultative

In just three sentences, you will reveal whether you are a consultative sales representative.

In the first sentence, a consultant identifies a customer problem in financial terms—what the problem is costing the customer, or what the customer could be earning without the problem. If you mention your product or service at this point, you are vending and not consulting.

In the second sentence, a consultant quantifies a profit improvement solution to the problem. If you mention your product or service at this stage, you are vending and not consulting.

In the third sentence, a consultant takes a position as manager of a problem-solving system and accepts single-source responsibility for its performance. In the course of defining the system in terms of contribution to customer profit, you will be able to mention products and services for the first time.

If you are selling as a consultant, it is easy to predict what the fourth sentence must be. It will be a proposal of partnership with your customer's top tier managers in applying your system to solve the customer's problem.

A consultant's problem-solving approach to selling requires helping customers improve their profit, not persuading them to purchase products and services. To solve a customer's problem, a consultant must first know the needs that underlie it. Only when a customer's needs are known can the expertise, hardware, and services that compose a system become useful components of their solutions. This is the difference between servicing a product and servicing a customer. It allows your relationships with customers to be consultative rather than the simple sell-and-bill relationship that characterizes traditional customer-supplier transactions at the vendor level.

The ideal positioning for a consultative seller is *customer profit-improver*. You can achieve this position by affecting one of a customer's operating processes in two ways: reducing its contribution to cost or increasing its contribution to sales revenues. A consultative seller's primary identification with profit improvement rather than with products, equipment, services, or even systems themselves gives the sales approach a decided economic cast. It focuses attention on the ultimate end benefit of a sale, not its components or cost. This gives you the same profit improvement objective as the top tier of your customer. It also professionalizes your mission by expressing it in business management terms, not sales talk.

Consultative Selling positions the seller as the vital ingredient in the selling process. It has become necessary to do this in one industry after another—and to convert product sales representatives into consultative sellers—because products and equipment have lost uniqueness in value. They have become commodities, parity products without differentiation from each other. As a result, they have lost premium value as the basis for their price.

To remain profitable, many suppliers have come to the realization that they must sell something more than commodity products. Product-related services provide part of the answer. But the major contribution to conferring premium value on a customer, and hence the major justification for charging a premium price, is *added value*—the value that can be added to a commodity product by a consultative seller who can apply it to improve customer profit.

Selling Return on Investment

From a top tier customer's point of view, a consultative sales representative is an integral part of every sale. Unlike product vendors, who are identified as a part of their own company and therefore do not go along with the sale of their product or service, consultative sellers are embedded in their systems and are "packaged" along with it. While a piece of equipment may endure longer than the equipment vendor, the consultative seller, in contrast, generally goes on making an important contribution to customer profit long after the original system has been installed. The seller's durability with a customer aptly defines the vital role a seller plays over and above the other elements of a consultative system.

A system sale is not the sale of products or equipment. Nor is it the sale of product-related services. It is not even the sale of the system itself. A system sale is the sale of a positive rate of return on the customer's investment; in short, *the economic effect of the system.*

Implicit in every system sale must be the assumption, held by seller and customer alike, that the system's return on investment (ROI) is undeliverable without the consultative seller. The consultant's personal intervention is central. It begins with prescribing the system and flows through its delivery, installation, coming on stream, continuing maintenance, periodic upgrading, and eventual replacement. As long as the consultant is perceived as the critical element, the system can hold together; it will not be "desystemized" into separate selective purchases made on the basis of competitive price. The consultant is the guardian of a system's premium price. If the consultant is unable to deliver a return on investment that justifies a premium price, the system will fall apart into its components.

In order to achieve a position as the single most important element in every system, a consultant must acquire two indispensable skills, unpracticed by typical vendors. One is the ability to plan customer profits. Systems require careful profit planning, not only in their prescription but also in their presentation, installation, and ongoing operation. The second skill is the ability to apply personal expertise to the customer's business.

Moving to a Consultative Approach

A consultative approach to selling is financial service selling. When a product-centered or equipment-oriented sales representative makes the transition to systems, three guidelines can help deemphasize the trained reliance on product. Applying these guidelines will profoundly affect your relationships with customers—in terms of what is sold, how it is sold, and how the customer perceives the value received in the relationship.

1. *Increase personalization of the relationship.* Product sales are based on performance of equipment. Systems sales are based on the performance of the consultative seller in partnership with top tier customers.

2. *Increase customer participation in the relationship.* Product sales are based on maximum seller participation and minimal customer participation. Consultative sales are based on a high degree of buyer-seller interaction at a customer's top and middle management tiers.

3. *Increase professionalization of the relationship.* Product sales are based on a traditional customer-vendor relationship. Consultative

sales are based on positioning the buyer as a client and the seller as a consultant.

Increasing Personalization

A system cannot be separated from its seller. The seller endows a system with personality. Of all its components, the seller becomes the indispensable operating element.

The increased amount of personalization required by consultative selling must be initiated by the consultant. The seller can become acknowledged as the system's leader only when the customer can perceive two truths:

1. The seller must become personally involved in understanding the customer's business function for which a system will be recommended. A requisite for this understanding is a close information-sharing relationship with the managers of each business function and the upper tier supervisors to whom they report.

2. The seller must become personally involved in creating the customer's profit improvement objectives and in applying the customer's system to achieve those objectives.

Increasing Customer Participation

Gaining acceptance as "process smart." The customer's process is the context for a consultative seller's systems. It is therefore essential that you become "process smart." This means learning all the aspects of customer processes that provide the basis for the successful creation, installation, and operation of your system. You must acquire this new knowledge firsthand, sleeves rolled up, right on the customer's premises. Both literally and figuratively, you must be willing to get dirty hands by touching the process and conducting give-and-take sessions with its operators, supervisors, and inspectors. There must be a demonstrated willingness to do this not just once but over and over again.

If you are going to be seen as genuinely understanding a customer's business, increased personal involvement with the customer's business functions must be geared toward adding factual knowledge about the customer's process, and psychological knowledge about the customer's needs and expectation of benefits.

Increasing factual knowledge. You will probably never know as much as customers do about their processes, and there is no need to. You must know more about *systems* that can improve the profit of their processes. To do this, you need facts about customer processes so that you can prescribe the most cost-effective system.

Encouraging psychological input. To be "process smart" means also to be "customer smart." Just as the consultative seller is the vital component of every system, the customer is the vital component of every process. Encouraging customer participation by asking for factual inputs is only one part of the story. You must also encourage the customer to discuss the psychological factors that influence the way the customer perceives the process, its peculiarities of performance, and the nature of the problems that reflect its unique personality. The customer's perception of an ideal solution to the problems must also be sought. Your system will have to address itself to these issues.

Increasing Professionalization

The client-consultant relationship, like the patient-doctor relationship, is a professional interaction. It involves far more trust than traditional customer-vendor relationships. To be a client, a customer must have confidence that it is safe to place proprietary process knowledge in a consultant's hands. A consultant-client relationship also involves a higher order of benefit; satisfactory product performance, which is generally the vendor's objective, is a minor benefit compared with profit improvement, which the consultative seller must deliver.

In addition to increased trust and a higher order of benefit, a consultant relationship differs from a vendor relationship in a third way: it is nonadversarial in nature. A seller positioned as a consultant does not compete against the client; they cooperate to help achieve client objectives. Instead of working in a win-lose situation, the consultant conducts a win-win relationship with the client. A second type of noncompetitiveness occurs in the special nature of the consultant's role. A customer can deal with many alternative vendors, but a client can deal with only one consultant for each business function. A seller can safeguard against competition by adequately fulfilling the consultant role.

The increased professionalism that characterizes a consultant-client relationship occurs when the consultant is able to do three things:

1. Set a profit improvement objective that meets client needs.
2. Establish a progressive schedule of work with the client to achieve that objective.
3. Construct a control procedure to ensure that the consultant's system is producing the promised profit on schedule.

Setting a profit improvement objective. The consultative seller must continually be alert to the needs that underlie customer objectives. Needs are generally connected to profits. Since you must function as a profit-improver, the financial implications of customer needs must be uncovered; these implications, in turn, provide the basis for customer objectives.

Establishing a work schedule. A consultative seller is performing professionally if the question "When?" is never asked by customers. The answer must always be ready before the question can be asked. You accomplish this by imposing a time frame on profit improvement, thus accommodating two sets of needs: your own need for enough time to do a thorough, professional job, and the customer's need to begin deriving benefits from your work.

Constructing controls. Work schedules run the risk of becoming fictional unless they can be controlled against straying off target or failing to produce their promised benefits. The natural appendage to every schedule must therefore be a set of control procedures. These procedures take two forms: on-plan/off-plan progress reports (no report is required if the schedule is being satisfactorily met), and periodic progress meetings.

Controls enable a client to develop a sense of security that needs will be met without undue risk of catastrophic failure. They are the foundation of the client's belief that it is safe to be a client. Without controls, a client reverts to being a customer.

Product Desensitization

The most difficult challenge to consultative sellers is to stop selling products and start selling the added financial values that they can contribute to a customer's business. This requires more than merely substituting one vocabulary for another; it means substituting one mindset for another. Before this can be done, however, you must first undergo a desensitization to traditional product affiliations.

Most sales representatives metamorphose into consultants through a two-stage process. The first stage is to forsake performance benefit orientation for financial benefit orientation. This is akin to the classic features-versus-benefits conversion that all vendors undergo. It is the next order of magnitude. But in Consultative Selling, performance benefits are insufficient reasons for a customer to buy. Performance benefits describe what a product *is;* they are its operating specifications. Consultative Selling requires a seller to describe what a system *does;* these are its financial specifications. It is the end accomplishment of a system's performance benefits that must be sold.

The second stage in translating performance benefits to financial benefits is the calculation of their dollar values. These values, referred to as incremental profits, are the consultative seller's stock in trade.

Product desensitization starts with awareness that systems selling is a translated dialog. All systems components, including the systems seller, must be translated into a customer value. Hanging out a laundry list of system components is meaningless unless their individual contribution to the customer's incremental profit is quantified. Mentioning product, elaborating on the technological superiority of equipment, extolling its construction characteristics or other qualities—all are meaningless unless their incremental contribution to the system's capability for profit improvement is quantified.

Translating product performance benefits into incremental profit benefits is the way consultants must think. "What is the contribution to customer profit?" is their key question. They sensitize themselves to bottom-line thinking because they have learned that intermediate-line thinking fails to accomplish two key objectives. It fails to position their customers as clients, since a client is a bottom-line beneficiary. And it fails to position themselves as consultants, since a consultant is a supplier of bottom-line benefits.

Nothing will deposition a seller from a consultative stance faster or more certainly than lapsing back to preoccupation with product. It is the consultative seller's deadliest sin and an ever-present pitall. At a customer's top tier, it can be fatal. The word "product" rather than "profit" lies poised from long habit on the tips of most vendors' tongues, ready to undo them. The best way to avoid slips of the tonuge is to learn to use the new frame of reference in parallel with the old one and translate as you go. Whenever a product is mentioned, define it immediately in terms of its contribution to customer profit. This is what customers do; they listen for the numbers. Consultative sellers must become sensitive to this need and deliver the benefit that customers seek: quantification of the dollar values they will receive, not enumeration of the products or their performance specifications.

Applying the 80–20 Rule

Preparation for Consultative Selling begins with identification of the customer accounts that are the best prospects for profit improvement. These accounts will be your principal source of profitable sales revenues. By concentrating on them, you will have your priority market segments pinpointed as major targets.

In every market, the familiar 80–20 rule will prevail: 80 percent of sales come from 20 percent of accounts. For consultative sellers, this means that only about 20 percent of all customers will contribute to profit heavily enough for them to become clients. Yet these relatively few customers will contribute as much as 80 percent of your profitable sales.

The 80–20 proportion is a generality. In some markets, it will require somewhat more than 20 percent of all customers to supply 80 percent of your profitable volume; in others, far less than 20 percent may do it. In this way, the 80–20 rule averages out.

Since client accounts will be those in the 20 percent category, the core of every consultative business is obviously quite small. This is a sobering fact. Every key account is precious; to lose one is to lose lifeblood. You must become as important to every key customer as the customer is to you. Only when you become a customer's preferred profit-improver can this happen. You must know more about the customer's processes than anyone else. And you must be able to supply profit-improving strategies to those processes better than any other seller.

Not all of your profitable sales volume will come from key accounts. If up to 80 percent of profit comes from 20 percent of accounts, then 20 percent of profit must come from the remaining 80 percent of accounts. This is good money; it need not be left on the table. But it will almost always be more expensive to earn, since its sources are far less concentrated, their needs for individualized treatment may be considerably greater, and they may not offer the same opportunity for repeat, high-volume follow-on sales.

For these reasons, you must create a different strategy in serving non-key accounts. In order to maximize profit, you should use a mix of two strategies. For the 20-percenters, sell as a consultant. For the 80-percenters, create standardized, ready-to-install, off-the-shelf systems; these can be cost-effectively sold or leased as commodities.

Converting Customers into Clients

A consultant cannot consult with a customer. A consultant requires a client: a customer with whom the consultant is a partner in profit improvement. Converting "customers" into "clients" is the major task for the consultative seller. In Consultative Selling, these two terms become interchangeable. (They are used interchangeably throughout the rest of this book, but "client" is always meant.)

If you allow a key account customer to remain a mere customer, you will be put at a serious disadvantage. The customer will treat you as an alternative vendor and will create a frankly competitive situation for you with rival suppliers. You will be forced to persuade the customer that your system delivers the best performance benefits, including the "best price."

In order to be a customer's *partner* in profit improvement, you must know what the customer knows—how profits are made in the customer's business and how they can be improved. Otherwise there will be nothing to partner about. Proud and professional vendors sometimes have difficulty in understanding this caveat. They believe they can partner by being "good old boys." They mistake friendship for partnership; they confuse camaraderie with clienthood. To be a partner, there is no alternative to learning the customer's business. As proof, every consultative seller has a database. It may be primitive, set up as the simple manual system shown in Figure 1-1. Two master folders each contain servant folders that store cost information for a customer's individual business functions and sales information for specific product lines and their markets.

Once a critical mass of data has been assembled, however, the manual system of storing and accessing customer information should be converted to an electronic database. An APACHE® database serves this purpose.* APACHE provides customer information in words, numbers, and graphic formats (such as computer-generated charts, tables, and diagrams) that can be directly incorporated into a consultant's Profit Improvement Proposals®. As with all consultative databases, APACHE databases all meet three requirements: they are industry-dedicated, operations-centered, and problem-oriented.

Industry-dedicated

If you serve a single industry, your database will be dedicated to that industry. If you serve multiple industries, you must have a sepa-

* APACHE® and Profit Improvement Proposal® are registered trademarks of Mack Hanan, owner of the copyright for the program entitled APACHE. This program is a computerized system for storing and accessing customer cost problems on a business function basis, as well as customer sales opportunities on a product-line, market-segment basis. When information on a supplier's systems capabilities is matched with customer data, APACHE can generate consultative Profit Improvement Proposals in billionths of seconds.

Figure 1-1. Startup manual database.

rately dedicated database for each industry just as if it were your only one. In this way, you replicate your customers' perceptions about the peculiarities, individualities, and idiosyncrasies of their businesses. You learn to think in the same industry terms that they do, keep alert to the same industry trends and conditions, understand the same industry constraints, and acquire similar industry sensitivities.

Operations-centered

If you serve one division or one function of your key customer businesses, the customer and the division or function are synonymous. Your database can be organized along division or functional lines. If you serve multiple types of divisional businesses or multiple business functions within your customer organizations, your database will have to be organized by specific lines of business and specific business functions for each customer. The customer is no longer definable in terms of the account as a whole. Instead, "the customer" is actually several individual operations managers, each of whose businesses you must know.

Problem-oriented

Each customer database must focus on the problems that will be your prime selling targets. These problems will conform to three criteria:

1. *They are important to your customers.* This means that, operationally and financially, they are adversely affecting customer productivity, denying added sales, and unnecessarily inflating costs.

2. *They will be profitable for customers to solve.* This means that the total cost of implementing a solution will be less than the continuing cost of tolerating the problem over a "useful life" of three to five years. It also means that the customer's profit from the solution must exceed or at least equal the profit from investing the same dollar resources in comparable alternative ways.

3. *They will be profitable for you to solve.* This means that you can sell the solution at a high margin. It also means that the solution will generate the improved customer profit you have promised so that you will be able to upgrade it and migrate it—and so that you will not have to deplete your margins by providing remedial service, repair, and replacement under warranty.

Incorporating the Solution

Into this mix of customer industry information, customer operations information, and customer problem information must be added the one element of information that is not derived from the customer: your solutions.

The act of inserting your solutions into a customer database on a problem-by-problem basis unifies the two businesses. It forms the basis for your partnership as problem-solvers.

Solutions should be entered into your customer database in two forms:

1. *Systems for solving customer problems.* Each product, service, and system you offer should be included as part of your internal information. Its features and benefits should be itemized, together with their synergistic effects when two or more products or services are combined in a system. Each system should be defined according to its regular and optional component parts. Every offering should be correlated to the customer business functions it affects. Sequential upgrading modules should be itemized so that the contribution of each product or system can be examined from its simplest state through its most comprehensive form. Customer business functions to which it can most naturally migrate should also be specified.

2. *System values.* Each product, service, and system should have four values attached to it. The first three are internally known. One is its cost to you. The second is its cost to your customers. The third is its resulting unit margin. The fourth value is external: the dollar value of the costs you can reduce in a customer's businesses or the dollar value of the new sales revenues you can help a customer attain.

These four sets of dollar values allow you to know if you are going to be able to meet the two major objectives of every key account sale. One is being certain that your customer will gain improved profit as a result of buying from you. The other is being certain that your own profit will be improved as a result of selling to your customer. If both profits can be improved, you have the basis for Consultative Selling.

Your problem-solving products and their values represent the corollary of your information on your customer's problems and their values. On the surface, it may seem that products from your side and dollars from the customer's side are being exchanged in a consultative sale. But your database will remind you that this is not the case. The actual exchange is a transfer of *values:* your customer's dollar values for your own dollar values. To say the same thing from a customer's point of view, a consultative sale is a trade of a customer's current costs plus the added costs of doing business with you for your near-term and future improvement of customer profits.

APACHE in Action

Dresser-Wayne is a manufacturer and marketer of management control systems for retail businesses. One of the major lines is a single-source system supplied to gasoline retail chains. It serves major oil company outlets and service stations, independent service stations, and convenience stores that also market gasoline. Its system consists of gas dispenser pumps, electronic control consoles that operate and monitor the pumps, automatic cash registers, automatic service equipment, and data storage and handling capabilities.

To the individual gas station retailer, the benefits of Dresser-Wayne's system are accurate cost control, inventory control, and reduced labor. Also, timely profit reports on sales provide the flexi-

Figure 1-2. Problem/opportunity summary.

Market Segment: Convenience stores
Customer: ABC Convenience Stores, Inc.
State/Region: New York/Northeast

	MONTHLY PROFIT CONTRIBUTION
OUTLET	
Credit control	$________
Inventory control	________
Cash control	________
Staff productivity	________
Maintenance	________
Throughput efficiency	________
Site layout/size	________
HOME OFFICE	
Data control and report	________
Cash management	________
Supervisor productivity	________
Communications	________
Total contribution/Month	$________
Total contribution/Year	$________

bility to change pricing quickly to correspond to peak and off-peak driving hours. In addition, the system safeguards against downtime and can lower space costs while increasing the throughput of customer traffic within the smaller space. The retailer's home office benefits too. It receives data on sales and inventory faster and more accurately. The data can be used to reduce costs and improve sales revenues by allowing improvements in the delivery schedules to each station. In addition, one supervisor at the head office can manage twelve stations instead of six, thereby saving supervisory labor costs.

The consultative sales force of Dresser-Wayne is equipped with an APACHE database on major oil companies, independents, and convenience stores. The general benefits that Dresser-Wayne can offer to all three segments are similar: improved profits through increased sales, and reduced costs with greater security and control. But the specific benefits vary with each market segment and each problem to be solved. Accordingly, APACHE is organized to allow a consultative sales representative to answer questions like these:

1. Where is the problem at the station level? Is it principally an inventory control problem based on ineffective cash management? Is it a credit control problem? Are receipts and distribution at the heart of the problem? Or is it a question of labor skills, quality of maintenance, or present station design and the resulting customer throughput?
2. Where is the problem at the home-office level? Data control and reporting? Cash management? supervisory management?
3. Is this an opportunity to sell a product, a comprehensive sys-

Figure 1-3. Problem analysis.

Market Segment: Convenience stores
Customer: ABC Convenience Stores, Inc.
State/Region: New York/Northeast
Business Function: Inventory control
Problem: Stock-out

	ANALYSIS
Average time out of stock	____________
Number of times out of stock per year	____________
Average number of gallons pumped per hour	____________
Margin per gallon (¢)	____________

tem, or perhaps a superproduct—several gas pumps, monitoring consoles, a cash management system, and a training program?

4. Is this a lease or a buy opportunity?

5. Is there an opportunity to sell a traffic-improvement plan to individual gas stations, or is it more cost-effective to focus on improving station profit contribution from existing layouts?

6. What are the total costs to be reduced? What are the total sales revenues to be gained? What are the investment offsets required to achieve these results? What net profit will result to the customer and to us? What is the return on investment?

APACHE reports on the total number of outlets that can be affected in each chain and identifies each as in the top 10 percent, in the middle, or among "all others." It specifies the average number of gallons each station moves each month, along with other products and services. Data are also included on each station manager's purchase preferences, work force, cost structure, and use of competitive equipment. Similar information is also available on home-office managers.

Consultative sales representatives at Dresser-Wayne consult with their APACHE before they consult with their customers. APACHE reveals the type of customer information that is partially shown in Figures 1-2, 1-3, and 1-4. These three figures are devoted to the convenience-store segment of Dresser-Wayne's market.

Figure 1-4. Benefit analysis.

Market Segment: Convenience stores
Customer: ABC Convenience Stores, Inc.
State/Region: New York/Northeast
Business function: Inventory control

	BENEFITS	
	$ Monthly	$ Weekly
Product loss		
Leakage	____________	____________
Vapor	____________	____________
Theft	____________	____________
Stock-out	____________	____________
Carrying excess inventory	____________	____________

On the problem/opportunity summary in Figure 1-2, a consultant has asked APACHE to show the monthly dollar profit currently being contributed by key functions and characteristics of stores in the ABC Convenience Stores chain located in New York. Some of these dollar values will be positive. Others will be negative contributions to profit. The positive values may indicate sales opportunities for Dresser-Wayne if they are lower than average. The negative values may indicate sales opportunities if they can be reduced or eliminated.

APACHE also shows the consultative seller the contributions to profit being made by four functions at the chain's home office. These may provide supplementary sales opportunities.

If the business function of inventory control, for example, shows a negative profit contribution or only a small positive contribution in Figure 1-2, it can be analyzed as a separate problem area as shown in Figure 1-3. The problem of stock-out can be intensively evaluated ac-

Figure 1-5. Equipment configuration analysis: present mix.

	Number per Year	Price	Annual Cost
Equipment			
Instrument A	______	______	______
Instrument B	______	______	______
Instrument C	______	______	______
Instrument D	______	______	______
Accessory Sets			
Set 1	______	______	______
Set 2	______	______	______
Set 3	______	______	______
Set 4	______	______	______
Materials			
Material XX	______	______	______
Material YY	______	______	______
Material ZZ	______	______	______

Figure 1-6. Financial analysis: present mix.

DEPRECIATION
Total annual instrument depreciation $__________
(Total # instruments × average price/useful life)

LEASE COST
Total annual instrument lease cost $__________
(Total # leased instruments × average lease cost/month × 12)

MAINTENANCE
Total annual instrument maintenance cost $__________
(Total # leased instruments × total # purchased instruments × average annual maintenance cost)

INTEREST ON PURCHASE PRICE
(Total # instruments purchased × average purchase price × cost of Money/100)

Figure 1-7. Equipment configuration analysis: optimal mix.

	Number per Year	Price	Annual Cost
Equipment			
Instrument A–B	______	______	______
Instrument C	______	______	______
Accessory Sets			
Set 1–2	______	______	______
Set 3	______	______	______
Materials			
Material XX	______	______	______
Material YY	______	______	______

cording to its gallonage and dollar values. If the consultant believes these values can be improved, APACHE will create a proposal to compare Dresser-Wayne's benefits with the customer's current situation. APACHE will then show Figure 1-4, pointing out the dollar benefits that the consultant can bring to the customer on a weekly and monthly basis for any individual store or for the entire ABC chain.

When Dresser-Wayne consultative sales representatives stand before their customers' top tier decisionmakers, they hold in their hands

Figure 1-8. Net benefit analysis: optimal mix.

	Optimal Mix	Present Mix
Expenses		
Depreciation	________	________
Equipment write-off	________	________
Lease cost	________	________
Maintenance	________	________
Interest on purchase price	________	________
Materials	________	________
Labor	________	________
Freight	________	________
Total Expense	________	________
Benefits		
Investment tax credit	________	________
Trade-in	________	________
Risk management	________	________
Financial risk reduction (opportunity cost)	________	________
Instrument standardization	________	________
Total Benefits	________	________
Net Expense	________	________
Net Benefit	________	________
Net Financial Benefit	________	________

a Profit Improvement Proposal. Its "product" is new profits for the customer.

Dresser-Wayne used to sell ironware: gas pumps and related equipment. Then its strategy was to sell groups of products and services called systems: not just gas pumps alone but control consoles, inventory gauges, automatic cash registers, and data modems together with some customer training and a lease program. Through Consultative Selling, Dresser-Wayne has transcended products, equipment, and systems to sell improved customer profitability. It has moved from a "hardware"-selling vendor that did business in iron, to a "software"-selling vendor that did business in data, to a retail management consultant that does business in helping its customers grow their own businesses.

Figures 1-5 through 1-8 show how a consultative seller in a very different business, scientific instruments, can work with APACHE to help optimize the mix and maximize the profit of a laboratory customer.

In Figure 1-5 the consultant asks APACHE to reach into its database and show the customer's current equipment configuration: instruments, accessory sets, and consumable materials. APACHE shows the four categories of costs that the customer incurs from the present mix (Figure 1-6). Taken together, these two figures give a bird's-eye view of the customer's laboratory function in terms of its hardware and software components and their costs. The consultant's challenge is clear: Can the customer be helped to do better?

In Figure 1-7, APACHE shows a more optimal mix of equipment for the customer, based on fewer categories of instruments and accessory sets. APACHE will create the net benefit analysis shown in Figure 1-8. This will become the focal point of the consultant's Profit Improvement Proposal.

2

How to Penetrate High Levels

Top tier customer management rarely deals with vendors, and then only under duress. They speak different languages. Vendors speak price and performance; management speaks value and profit. Vendors speak of their competitors; management is concerned about its own. Vendors wonder when management will ever buy; management wonders when vendors will ever leave.

Vendors who stand before their customer's top tier will not do so for long, or soon again. For consultative sellers to make a stand, and make it again and again, they must be prepared to speak the language of management, address customer concerns instead of their own, and put to work their knowledge of the customer's business so that a demonstrable improvement—not just a shipment of goods—takes place.

Key account sales representatives who want to penetrate the top customer tier must position themselves to discuss, document, and deliver their answers to the question, "How much profit will you add?" That must be their mission; it is what being a consultative sales representative is all about. (This is illustrated in Figure 2-1.)

To take the consultative position requires three skills. One is knowing the customer's business well enough to know how a profit is made. A second skill is demonstrating an improvement. The third skill is creating close, continuing partnerships on the top tier that foster ongoing knowledge of the customer's business and renewed opportunities to improve it.

The key account representatives who stand as consultants assume a hybrid stance. They are not vending, so they cannot be positioned as

Figure 2-1. Customer decisionmaker hierarchy.

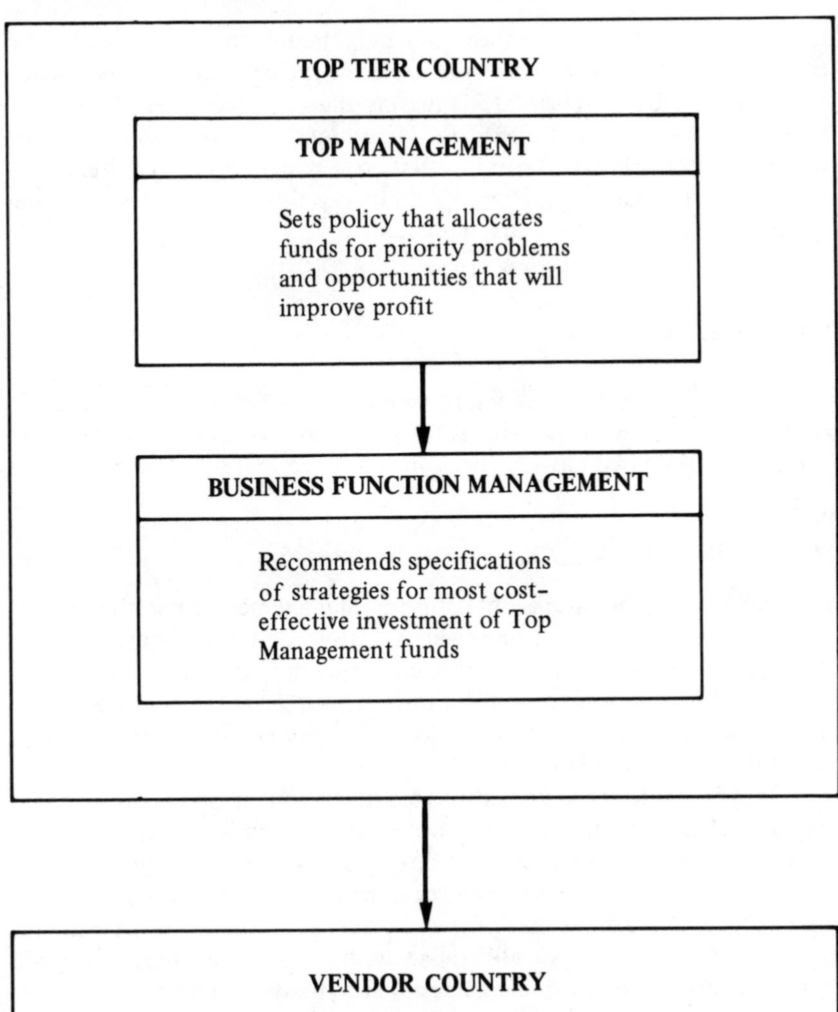

traditional sellers. Nor are they managing their customer's business, so they cannot be positioned as peers. Above the one, they are below the other. Their closest correlate is among the customer's own staff, not with anyone else from the outside. Their most approximate role models are internal people who report to the top tier, who bring to it financially quantified solutions for proposal and disposal, and who must then implement them when they are budgeted.

The Four-Act Play

Internal managers often approach their top tier as the principals in a four-act play. Key account sales representatives would do well to follow this scenario closely, both in sequence and in content.

Act I: "Why Do You Want to See Me?"

Everyone who approaches top tier management must offer justification. Management's brainpower is every company's most precious resource, and it must be profitably engaged every minute. Downtime is time lost forever. Management knows what is profitable and asks, Do you? Management knows what needs improvement to become more profitable and asks, Do you?

In your role as a consultative seller, you must be prepared to declare what you want to see customer decisionmakers about. It must be either a problem of significant cost or a major revenue opportunity, and it must be solvable within a reasonable period of time. Issues that meet these criteria are the proper business of top tier management. Any other issues—especially those within your own business—will bring the response that management is too busy with its own business to deal with them. Act I can be the final act unless the customer's business is spotlighted on center stage.

Act II: "What Do You Want Me to Do About It?"

Management-level decisionmakers make decisions; they do not conceptualize or contemplate idly. You cannot raise an issue with management merely to provoke intellectual curiosity; you must offer a remedy. Once management knows why you want its attention, it next must know what you want it to do. In the end it is you, of course, who will end up doing something about the issues you have raised. But customer management must do something first: It must appropriate assets in the form of dollars and people.

Assets are allocated for solutions, to prevent or relieve problems. Management must be told what solutions are available. Some may already have been tried and failed. Should any of them be considered anew? Some attempts may already be in implementation. Can they be reinforced? Should they be superseded before they fail or prove cost-ineffective? Is there a best solution; if so, how can we tell it is best? What can its contribution be expected to amount to?

When customer management evaluates solutions, it is not evaluating products, services, or systems. It may know little about them and care less. Top management assesses only the financial results of a solution, not its components or their performance. Operating managers will be interested in systems, but at the top, the dialog of Act II will be principally in dollar terms: how much profit you are prepared to offer management and how much, in return, you want as your reward.

Act III: "How Do I Know It Will Work?"

If management likes what you want it to do—in other words, if it likes the amount of added profit you want it to be able to make—it will want to know how it can realize your proposal. "How do I know the profits you promise will actually accrue?" That is what top management means by "will it work?" It is not a question of whether the gears will mesh or the system will integrate; these performance benefits will have to be demonstrated to operating management. Throughout the top tier, a proposal works when it produces the profit that you claim for it. If it operates mechanically, chemically, or electronically but the profits are not forthcoming, it does not work.

Act III is where you must attest to the workability of your solution. You must document the profits, showing their source, their flow over time, and their cumulative total. You must also document your system: What major components will it contain? What is their contribution to improved profit? How do they conform to state-of-the-art technology, and what are their track records?

Act III can therefore be divided into two sequential scenes. First, you must strike a partnership with managers of customer business functions on the performance contributions of your proposals. Then, when a consensus agreement has been reached at this operating level, the financial contributions should be proposed to top management. This bottom-up phasing of approval permits top management to obtain the immediate concurrence of its operating decisionmakers: "Is this what you want? Will it work the way they say it will?'' It also prevents resentment at the operating levels; instead of having a decision handed down, they will participate in handing it up.

Act IV: "When Do We Get the Show on the Road?"

When key account sales representatives sell consultatively, the call to action will most likely come from the customer in Act IV. As soon as your solution is perceived to work financially and operationally, top management will want to implement it. Time is money. Every minute's delay deprives them of promised profits.

Implementation consists of four elements. The first three concern what will be installed, when it will become operational, and who from each side will be involved. The fourth element is the sum total of the first three: What resources will have to be provided from the customer's business to match the resources contributed by you and your support services? Only when money and people—their time and talent—are allocated does something get done in business. You must be prepared to specify what both parties will have to put up in order to get the show on the road.

Key account representatives must be trained to produce their four-act plays at a fast clip, requiring a minimum of props and moving smoothly from one act to the next. Like all good plays, consultative proposals should be presented orally, with a copy of the libretto left behind for each member of the audience. An hour, allowing time for interruptions, is the maximum length any performance should take. The audience has other plays to go to.

Where are the trap doors under top management's carpet? Everywhere. Act I can close out your performance if you focus on a problem that customer management does not perceive as significant or if you fail to describe a truly significant problem correctly in management terms. You will be dismissed as not understanding the customer's business.

If the solution you propose in Act II pays out too little profit or is too late in coming, it may be rejected. If it is too great in amount, your credibility may be suspect—can you really do what you say you can do? If you are deemed not to be credible, you will not be trusted with management's approval. Even worse, if your solution appears to be unlikely and you provide supportive testimony from another company or another industry, you may be summarily dismissed as not understanding the differences between your customer's business and all others.

If fault is found with your financial documentation of profit contribution in Act III, especially if the errors are in your favor, your image or your credibility will be downgraded. You may nonetheless survive if the corrected contribution remains significant. If your profit analysis fails utterly, you will be dismissed as not understanding the first thing about the business of consultation in profit improvement: how to measure profits.

Act IV is the proof of the pudding. If you cannot implement, you will be dismissed as not understanding the second thing about your business: how to bring new profits in.

Five-Stepping the Consultative Selling Cycle

A key account sales representative going through the Consultative Selling cycle will take five steps. They are all forms of learning and teaching. The cycle contains two types of elements. Planning the account's penetration and generating the proposal are the least time-consuming elements. But the other three elements are dependent on people inside the customer organization: their cooperation, their information, and their instigation of acceptance within the company. When the selling cycle turns over slowly, people problems are probably the reason. This puts a premium on your ability to achieve multiple partnerships with operating, financial, and managerial levels in your accounts.

The five-step selling cycle starts with databasing and proceeds to penetration planning, preliminary partnering, proposing, and implementing. As logic suggests, they are generally sequential. Frequently, however, databasing must be returned to, planning must be revised, and initial partnerings must be reinstituted with different influencers or decisionmakers. In these instances, the cycle is less of a progressive curve than a zigzag.

1. *Databasing*. Knowledge of the customer's business is the basis for penetration planning, partnering, and proposing. Two things can usually be said about it. Unlike product knowledge, customer knowledge is generally sparse. And, again unlike product knowledge, it requires getting into the customer's business by knowing the determinants of customer profit: how customer business functions can cost less to operate and how customer markets can become better sources of profitable revenues.

2. *Penetration planning*. The database predetermines the penetration plan you develop for each key account and the partnering and

proposing you will employ to execute it. That is why Consultative Selling is data-dependent. The penetration plan deals with data on an *as-if* basis: as if the data *are* the customer's business, as far as your sales opportunity is concerned. The plan then asks—and answers—the following questions:

What is your optimal solution for each customer problem and opportunity? What is its dollar value to the customer? To you? What is it composed of—what systems of products and services? Who are the decisionmakers involved? Taking all your solutions together, what is the total profit contribution you can make to this customer this year? What is the customer's total expected profit contribution to you? What is your revenue-to-expense ratio to achieve it?

The penetration plan is your operating manual with each account. It should serve two purposes. It will allow you to manage the account's penetration, determining how much of its potential contribution you are reaching, whether or not you are on schedule, and what unexploited opportunities remain for proposing. This is the plan's internal function. It should have an external use as well. It should be positioned with your customer as your mutual profit partnership plan. Each consultant should prepare each account's plan with customer participation, making sure that its priorities and assumptions match those of the customer. The consultant should be equally certain that customer decisionmakers understand how much profit improvement to expect and what their own commitment of resources will have to be if they want it.

3. *Preliminary partnering*. Partnering begins when key account representatives share their penetration plans with customer decisionmakers and influencers. These may include division and department managers, financial administrators, functional managers in sales, engineering, and manufacturing, and other operating managers.

With each category of management, mutual objectives must be established and agreements reached on the most cost-effective strategic approach to achieve them. Information must be encouraged to flow both ways so that everybody contributes something to your customer database and everybody takes something away, only to return it in more accurate, fact-enriched form.

Partners will emerge in several guises. Information partners will show and tell but do nothing. Action partners will work with you but will not necessarily go to bat for you. On the other hand, advocate-type partners will speak for you at high management levels but will play no active role in getting the work done. Somewhere along the line, you will be able to identify you mentor partners, the coaches who will guide you through the customer's political and social systems, steering you toward supporters and away from delayers or apparent nay-sayers.

Partnering at many different position levels, with many different personalities in a wide range of occupational and political relationships, is a complex task. It is the master skill of consultative sales representatives. Unless you can identify your mission with each potential partner's own objectives and create a participative strategy that takes those objectives into consideration, you will essentially be reduced to vending, no matter what other skills you may possess.

4. *Proposing*. Each major proposal to improve a key account's profit or productivity should be one of the modules in the penetration plan. It should bear a priority ranking and, whenever possible, flow out of a previous proposal and into a following one. The knowledge of what to propose, to whom, and when, must come out of customer partnering.

Your customer database is your inanimate "proposal partner." In communion with it, you can call up the optimal solution to customer problems and opportunities by reviewing a range of solutions. Some may have been proposed previously to solve similar problems. You can also mix and match the piece parts of two or more solutions, playing a "What if?" game: What if we add this from here and subtract that from there; how does it affect our ability to improve customer profit?

If there are optional solutions, each should be worked up so it can be discussed with your customer partners. Even if there is only one clear-cut solution, it should be preproposed to customer partners so that their input, and their support, can be obtained. When the proposal is actually presented, there must be no surprises between you and your customer partners.

Each proposal should be looked on as serving three purposes. The first is to sell at a high-margin price that is commensurate with the customer's improved profit. Second, a proposal should prepare the way for its follow-on proposals. Third, successful proposals should be recycled into your database so that they can be used over and over again as references for proposals yet to come.

5. *Implementing*. Proposals are born in data. They either mature profitably or perish in implementation. No matter how optimal your solutions may be, they are valueless if their integration into the customer's business falls short of the full profit contribution you have proposed.

Implementation is the acid test of your ability to convert promise into performance. It is your main chance to cement partnerships, earn your way into further learning about the customer's business, and be first in line to propose your next strategy to improve customer profit.

No matter what business you are in, and no matter what specific aspects of integrating your solutions you must observe, there are three common denominators of implementation to which you must adhere.

First, as quickly as possible you must install your solution in the customer's operations. It must start to function, and it must begin to produce the profit stream you have proposed. The onset of profit is the crucial element of implementation. Every day of delay—in many situations, every hour and every minute—has a dollar equivalent that subtracts from the promise of your proposal. Conversely, every day of earlier profit is a bonus.

Monitoring your solution—not just its operating performance but also its delivery of improved profit—must go hand in glove with installation. You and your customer partners will have to agree beforehand on the criteria for monitoring (exactly what is expected) and the milestones (exactly when it is due).

Finally, there can be no implementation without training the customer's people to operate the solution, maintain it, and measure its contribution. Training helps guarantee the achievement of your proposals. It spares your customer added cost, thereby increasing profit. Similarly, it also spares you the added cost of providing service, repairs, and replacement parts due to customer ineptitude, costs that can seriously injure your own profit on sales.

The beginning point of every Consultative Selling cycle is clear: It is always databased. But when does a cycle end? It is tempting to say that customer acceptance of your proposal is the natural end point. But getting the customer's improved profits to flow is really the signal that your original promise is on the way to realization and that you have earned the right to propose once again, initiating a new cycle as the next stage of an endless sequence of profit improvement proposals.

3

How to Merit High Margins

For both consultative sellers and customers, profit is the name of the game. While the game is the same, the role you play in it is very different from that of your customer.

Setting profit objectives is the customer's business. It cannot be abdicated, nor can the customer delegate it to anyone outside the company. No one who is external to a company can ever know enough about total corporate assets and liabilities—financial, operational, or human—to set business objectives based on them. Besides, your concern with the customer's business is rarely an overall one. It is concentrated on the product and service systems, and their market segments, with which you yourself are involved. As a result, your role is concerned with the additive effects that your product and service systems can have on the customer's profitability. You are his incremental profit-improver, not his total profit-maker.

A customer's primary management function is to develop strategic and tactical plans that can achieve profit maximization. Your role is limited to profit betterment. This means that you will propose your contribution from the point at which customers have finished developing their own profit plans. The end point of the customer's profit objectives becomes your point of departure.

Generating Profit Improvement Proposals

A consultative seller's day-to-day work is the generation of Profit Improvement Proposals, referred to as PIPs. Each PIP adds value to your customer's profit objectives, through the application of your product and service systems to the customer's business. By doing so, you are able to merit added margin in return.

The process of generating profit proposals must be a continuing one. Once it begins, it can go on without end because the profit improvement opportunities in a customer company are limitless.

You will find the task of selecting your profit improvement portfolio easier if you apply five criteria. They will steer you toward Profit Improvement Proposals that have the greatest chance of succeeding.

1. *New profits should be achievable within an average of 90 days.* Longer time frames incur unpredictable risks; they not only defy ready calculation but invite disenchantment or cancellation.

2. *New profits should be significant for both you and your customer.* Shared profit improvement should not be confused with equal profit. The first objective—profitability for both—is a vital aspect of the concept of partnership. The second—equal profit—is both impossible and unnecessary.

3. *New profits must draw on a major product or service capability* of your company if it is to be profitable for you. Similarly, in order for your customer to profit, your proposals must affect a major product, service, or operation.

4. *New profits must be measurable* in terms of a net increment or a decremental investment in operating assets. If it cannot be measured, or if no provision is made to quantify it, agreement on whether it even took place may be impossible to obtain.

5. *New profits should not be an isolated entity* but a module that leads naturally to the next infusion of profit and then to the next one after that.

Three Types of Profit Improvement Proposals

Profit Improvement Proposals are the basic sales tools for key account penetration. They are designed to permit you to sell at high-profit margins to high customer levels. Frequently they are tailored for specific high-level decisionmakers to reflect their functional or personal perspective. In all cases, they identify you as being in a financial service business that affects the bottom line of a customer's business—the fundamental consultative positioning. There are three types of Profit Improvement Proposals.

Entry proposals. When you penetrate a customer's business for the first time, or penetrate a new business function within the same customer account, you should construct a proposal that will guarantee successful entry. First proposals must deliver. For this reason, they should be conservative both in the amounts of improved profit they promise and in the time frames they allow for its inflow. Showing speedy results is the paramount consideration, demonstrating in the shortest possible time that profit can be improved. This dictates that you should select an entry problem whose scope you can limit and whose forthcoming solution you can vouch for at the highest level of confidence.

Mainstay proposals. Core strategies for customer penetration are the mainstays of your annual plan. These are your bread-and-butter proposals designed to solve comprehensive customer problems and deliver major amounts of profits to both of you as their reward. As a group, they should yield about 80 percent of your annual profit contribution to each account and a similar proportion of each account's contribution to you. When this occurs, you will know that you are managing your key accounts "according to plan."

Opportunity proposals. No matter how well you plan, opportunities will rise up in the course of your progressive penetration of each customer. The solution of one problem almost always reveals another. The success of one solution almost always provokes customer interest in another application somewhere else.

As your customer database grows, more opportunities to propose will become available. Even though you have not planned them, you should keep on your toes for the chance occurrences that invite a proposal. When they come, you can structure a solution for them. Some of these opportunities will be entry proposals. Others can turn into mainstay proposals that open up entire new areas of profitability.

All three types of proposing need to take into consideration four guidelines: following the proper sequence for the proposal, justifying high margins, partnering with top tier decisionmakers to implement the proposal, and migrating initial sales success.

The Proposal Process

Proposing is a three-step process: definition of a customer problem to be solved or a customer opportunity to be capitalized on; prescription of the profit improvement benefit from solving the problem or capitalizing on the opportunity; and description of the operational and financial workings of the system that can yield the improved profit.

Step 1: Problem/Opportunity Definition

Your initial task is to establish consultant credibility. Initial credibility comes only from displaying knowledge of a customer's business. Until a customer can say, "That salesperson knows my business," the customer will rarely be inclined to say, "That salesperson can improve my profit."

In fact, you must be knowledgeable about two areas of a customer's business. First, you must know the location of significant cost centers that are susceptible to reduction. Second, you must know how a customer's customers can be induced to buy more from the customer. In the first instance, you must prescribe a system that will reduce customer costs. This is a problem-solving system. In the second instance, you must prescribe a system that will increase customer sales. This is an opportunity system.

Defining a customer problem or opportunity has two parts: what you know, and how you know it. The second part documents the first by citing the sources of your knowledge. It also reinforces your credibility. There are three likely sources of knowledge about a customer cost problem or sales opportunity. One is that the customer revealed it. This is the "horse's mouth" source. A second source of knowledge is past experience with the customer, with other companies in the same industry, or "track record." Or knowledge can come from homework. This is the "midnight oil" source.

Step 2: Profit Improvement Prescription

The objective of the first step in a consultative presentation is to say to a customer, in effect: "You have a situation that is detrimental to your profit. Either you are incurring unnecessary costs or you are failing to capture available sales revenues." The objective of the second step is to say, "Working together, we can reduce some of those costs or gain some of those sales at a cost-beneficial investment."

In this way, you further reinforce the perception of being knowledgeable about the customer's business by framing the system's benefit in businesslike terms of return on investment. By quantifying an added value the system can make to the customer's operations, you are creating a business-manager-to-business-manager context for customer decisionmaking, in contrast to a vendor-to-purchaser context.

The prescription for customer profit improvement must specify the positive return that can predictably result from installation of your system. The return should be specified as both a percentage rate of improvement and its equivalent in dollars. These quantifications, the end-benefit specifications in money terms, rather than specifics about the system's performance or components, are the ultimate specifications of the consultant's system. These are what a customer will or will not buy. They are therefore what you must prescribe for delivery.

IBM consultants approach top tier management of key retail customers in a model consultative fashion on behalf of IBM's computer-assisted checkout station. The consultants prescribe profit improvement benefits of reduced costs and increased sales like this: "For a store with gross weekly sales of $140,000, savings are projected at $7,651 a month by faster customer checkout and faster balancing of cash registers." The time required to check out an average order is said to be reduced by almost 30 percent. In addition, IBM sales representatives claim that the elimination of time and cost expenses of correcting checker errors can contribute annual savings of more than $91,000 per store.

If a store is growing, its total savings every year can approach one week's gross sales at the $140,000 level. The net value of these savings falls directly to the store's bottom line. The essential contribution made by IBM is providing added growth funds that supplement revenues from sales and can be invested for still further growth.

IBM regards a customer's checkout function as a "mix" of several operations and their attendant costs. It seeks to reduce the cost contribution the mix makes to customer profits. All customer business functions operate through mixes. Some mixes are simply conglomerations of products. Others contain services, such as training or maintenance. Still others are composed of systems that, in turn, are composed of subsystems. You will have to determine the mix into which you fit, what you can contribute in "hardware" and "software," and what dollar values of improvement you can propose. The mix becomes your market; it is where you sell. Even more, it must become the area of your expertise. You must know how to make it contribute to profits in the most cost-effective manner. You must know this better than anyone else. You must master the operation of the mix so well that you can present yourself to your customers as their industry's "mixmaster."

Customer mixes usually lag behind the optimal mix. They frequently represent a sizable investment. They also are tied to a customer's learning curve. Customer people have learned how to operate their current mix; they have become familiar with its capabilities and its quirks. Training programs have been built around it. Psychologically, it has become "the way we do things around here." For all these reasons, a current mix is hard to change, in spite of a promise to make it more optimal.

Penetration with a changed mix can be made only if there is a reason to change it that is more powerful than all the reasons not to change it. Improved productivity and profits are bottom-line reasons to change. They have more meaning than appeals to "be first," "be modern," "be competitive," or "be positioned for the future." The appeal that can win must be the appeal to "be more profitable now."

Customers know how easily improved profits can be consumed by the price of change, even for an admittedly more optimal mix. As a result, consultative sales representatives will have to surround their financial benefits with supplementary benefit values. First, they must provide a training program to teach customer people how to obtain the full financial benefits of their new mix. Second, they must provide service, maintenance, and a repair, replacement, and restocking program so that the operation of the new mix can be continuous and free from downtime. Third, they must be supported by a broad base of industry data on the performance and profitability characteristics of the type of mix they propose. This will help them be perceived as working from a credible source, have ready answers to customer questions, and act as professional instructors in the management of its profit contribution.

In order to improve a customer's mix, you will have to improve its ability to contribute higher profits or greater productivity. There are three ways you can accomplish this objective:

1. *Supplant* one or more elements in the current mix. If the mix is labor-intensive, you may be able to reduce its cost by substituting an automated process or eliminating an operation altogether. Or you may be able to combine several processes, eliminating their overlapping costs.

2. *Substitute* your product or process for a competitive product or process that is part of the current mix. The basis for your recommendation must be that improved financial benefits will accrue to the customer if the mix is altered, not simply that more advantageous performance benefits will be realized.

3. *Restructure* the mix in such a significant manner that you will be the sole knowledgeable expert in its revamped composition, operation, and contribution to improved profits. Your identification as the sole source, or at least the originating source, of a new functional approach can help pull through your penetration, as well as make it easier to push. In addition to the improvement in profits from becoming your partner, the prestige of working with you as the industry innovator can provide an extra motivation for customers to become partners.

Step 3: System Definition

The third presentation step is to define the system that will deliver the promised profit improvement mix and to justify its premium price by interpreting price in terms of investment in the new mix. Customers must not be asked to buy systems; you must invite them to improve profit. They are not quoted a system's price; you must promise them a positive return on the investment in their system.

The purpose of defining the system is not to sell it. Rather, it is to present a system package as a form of proof that the promised benefit is derived from known capabilities that have been prescribed precisely because they will contribute in the most cost-beneficial way to the customer's profit improvement. The system substantiates your promise. Its capabilities, plus your personal expertise in applying them, are the means of conferring new profitability on the customer.

Price is an intimate part of a system. It is the single most revealing component. Not only does it have high visibility, it also possesses high connotative power. Premium price connotes premium value. It conveys more than the system's cost; it communicates the system's value.

Premium price can be justified by a system's ability to deliver premium value. If price contributes to value by assuring a system's profit-improving quality, and if price can be recovered by a return on investment that exceeds it, a premium price is justified.

Since system price depends on a customer's improved profit, system pricing is value pricing. The definition of value in terms of the amount by which profit is actually improved will always vary from customer to customer. As a result, there is no such fixed item as "system price," even for the same system. Price will be proportional, therefore, to the degree of value contributed by a system.

A model system presentation outline is shown in Figure 3-1. As a Profit Improvement Proposal of this type is progressively presented, it should make successive claims on a customer's propensity to buy. Defining a customer problem or opportunity should condition a customer to relate to you as a business manager. The next presentation step, prescribing a quantified benefit, should condition a customer to regard the system as a profit-making investment, not as a cost or a collection of components. Defining the system and justifying its price should condition a customer to credit the prescription as believable and achievable.

The final step in a system's presentation is to set down the standards by which you will progressively monitor the system's ability to

Figure 3-1. A proposal to improve the profit of Trickle River Canyon Power Company.

CHASTE WASTECORP

(1) Problem to Be Solved

Cost-effective disposal of low-level radioactive waste.

(2) Prescription to Solve the Problem

Improve profit by reducing annual costs of handling low-level radioactive waste by more than $400,000 and simultaneously maintain complete safety together with full legislative compliance.

(3.1) Solution System

1. AECC volume-reduction system
   - 1.1 Handles all plant-generated liquid wastes.
   - 1.2 Twenty to fifty gallons per hour; will handle a two-unit plant.
   - 1.3 Produces dry free-flowing product.
   - 1.4 Automatic, remote operation including system. Decontamination for maintenance.
   - 1.5 Non-mechanical fluid bed dryer.
2. Licensability * consultation services
3. Technical support services
   - 3.1 Inspection of equipment during storage—refurbishment if required.
   - 3.2 Live-in engineering consultation during installation.
   - 3.3 Training of operating and maintenance personnel.
   - 3.4 Live-in engineering consultation during startup.
   - 3.5 Engineering participation during demonstration test.
4. Equipment supply contract services
5. Maintenance contract services
6. Total project management consultation service to concentrate single-source responsibility provided by Chaste Wastecorp profit improvement team
7. Access to our information bank on radiation-waste disposal

* Topical Report AECC-1-A; approved by NRC, December 1975.

Figure 3-1 (*continued*).

(3.2) Solution System Rate of Return

Accounting rate of return =	29.2%
Cost savings/year =	+$400,000

Incremental Investment

Cost of equipment	$1,000,000
Installation	200,000
Building space penalty	200,000
Total cost	$1,400,000

Operating Costs (Dollars in $000)

Costs	*Present System*	*Proposed System*
Labor	$120	$ 25
Material	200	11
Transportation and burial	280	70
Maintenance	20	30
Power	1	20
Depreciation	40	96
Totals	$661	$252

Proposed Annual Savings = $409,000

$$\frac{409{,}000}{661{,}000} = 61.9\%\ \text{Cost reduction benefit}$$

Profitability Evaluation

Accounting Rate of Return

Total investment	$1,400,000	
Annual savings before tax	409,000	
Annual savings after 48% tax	212,000	
Rate of return		15.1%

Cash-Flow Payback (W/O Escalations)

1. Savings after tax = $212,000 per year
2. Straight-line depreciation (4% per year) = $56,000
3. Investment-tax credit (10%) = $140,000 (2nd year)
   Cash payback by end of 5th year (4 years, 9 months)

deliver the promised benefit in partnership with the customer. At least three control standards should be set so that a working partnership can be confirmed between consultant and customer:

1. Time frames for the accomplishment of each installation and operational stage.
2. Checkpoints for measuring the impacts of phasing the system into customer business functions.
3. Periodic progress review and report sessions to head off problems and anticipate new applications and opportunities for system extension, upgrading, modernization, and replacement.

In Figure 3-2, a four-stage profit improvement approach is shown for a materials cleaning system for metal, plastic, and rubber parts.

At Stage 1 the total incremental investment required by purchase and installation of the system is itemized. Stage 2 sets down the annual contribution to profit improvement that the system can make, in terms of a net decrease in operating cost.

Stage 3 has two parts. Part A shows the effect of the system on operating costs. In Part B the consultant can demonstrate the effect of the system on revenues. Finally, in Stage 4 the system's profit return is figured in relation to the incremental investment required to obtain it.

Figure 3-2. A four-stage profit improvement approach.

STAGE 1. INCREMENTAL INVESTMENT ANALYSIS

1. Cost of proposed equipment	$39,600		
Estimated installation cost	6,000		
Subtotal	$45,600		
Minus initial tax benefit of	3,190		
Total		$42,410	1
2. Disposal value of equipment to be replaced	8,000		
Capital additions required in absence of proposed equipment	6,000		
Minus initial tax benefit for capital additions of	420		
Total		$13,580	2
3. Incremental investment (1 — 2)		$28,830	3

Figure 3-2 (*continued*).

STAGE 2. PROFIT IMPROVEMENT ANALYSIS (ANNUAL CONTRIBUTION)

4. Profit improvement — net decrease in operating costs (from line 27)	$24,952	4
5. Profit improvement — net increase in revenue (from line 31)	$	5
6. Annual profit improvement (lines 4 + 5)	$24,952	6

STAGE 3. NEXT YEAR OPERATING BENEFITS FROM PROPOSED EQUIPMENT

A. Effect of proposed equipment on operating costs

(Computed on Machine-Hour Basis)	*Present*	*Proposed*	
7. Direct labor (wages plus incentives and bonuses)	$ 10.50	$ 3.50	7
8. Indirect labor (supervision, inspectors, helpers)	3.67	1.22	8
9. Fringe benefits (vacations, pensions, insurance, etc.)	2.15	0.72	9
10. Maintenance (ordinary only, parts and labor)	1.18	0.90	10
11. Abrasives, media, compounds, or other consumable supplies	1.32	1.10	11
12. Power	0.56	0.48	12
13. Total (sum of 7 through 12)	$ 19.38	$ 7.92	13
14. Estimated machine hours to be operated next year	2,400	3,000	14
15. Partial operating costs next year (13 × 14)	$46,512 (A)	$23,760 (B)	15
16. Partial operating profit improvement (15A — 15B)		$22,752	16

Figure 3-2 (*continued*).

(Computed on a Yearly Basis)	*Increase*	*Decrease*	
17. Scrap or damaged work	$	$ 700	17
18. Down time		1,500	18
19. Floor space			19
20. Subcontracting			20
21. Inventory			21
22. Safety			22
23. Flexibility			23
24. Other			24
25. Total	$ (A)	$ 2,200 (B)	25
26. Net decrease in operating costs (partial) (25B — 25A)		$ 2,200	26
27. Total effect of proposed equipment on operating costs (16 + 26)		$24,952	27

B. Effect of proposed equipment on revenue

(Computed on Yearly Basis)	*Increase*	*Decrease*	
28. From change in quality of products	$	$	28
29. From change in volume of output			29
30. Total	$ (A)	$ (B)	30
31. Net increase in revenue (30A — 30B)		$	31

STAGE 4. ANALYSIS OF RETURN ON INCREMENTAL INVESTMENT

32. Incremental investment (line 3)	$28,830	32
33. Annual profit improvement (line 6)	$24,952	33
34. Before-tax return on investment (line 33 ÷ line 32)	86%	34

A projected profit improvement of approximately $25,000 means a before-tax rate of return of roughly 86 percent. This earmarks an exceptionally good opportunity for the consultant to propose.

As Figure 3-2 shows, the consultant has taken three stages to get to the point where a number can be put on the value contributed by the system. At Stage 1, the total incremental investment required by purchase and installation of the system is itemized. Stage 2 sets down the annual contribution to profit improvement that the system can make. Sometimes this contribution will take the form of a net increase in revenue. In this case it comes from a net decrease in operating costs. In Stage 3, operating costs can be expected to come largely from a decrease in customer downtime as well as reduced scrap or damaged work. Savings will also be derived from reduced costs of labor, fringe benefits, maintenance, and power.

A shorter format for a cost-benefit analysis to calculate a system's return is shown in Figure 3-3.

How to Price a Customer's Profit Improvement

To endow systems with a premium price, you must provide customers with financial proof of a premium benefit. By selling the system's profit improvement instead of its components, you provide your customers with the rationale they need to endorse the system's required investment. Price then appears to be a function of return on investment, not a function of cost.

Valuing the Increment

The profit improvement approach to pricing provides a means of valuing the benefit of a system's use in specific dollar amounts of incremental profit. It compares the profit improvement benefits the customer can anticipate to the investment required to obtain them. Return on investment is the most meaningful way to measure the value that is received for each dollar that is expended. It is therefore an exceedingly persuasive selling tool.

Return-on-investment pricing is a measuring rod for evaluating the improved profit contribution that a system can make to a customer. In terms of return on investment, a customer's improved profit can be defined as the ratio of *incremental income earned* to *incremental cost* of the system (*price* and any other *added capital invested* in obtaining the system).

ROI-Connected Price

The return-on-investment basis for pricing relates price to a system's impact on customer profit. Rather than base price on cost, the ROI approach connects price to the customer's improved profits.

Figure 3-3. Cost-benefit analysis.

Incremental Investment	
1. Cost of proposed equipment	$______
2. *Plus:* Installation costs	______
3. *Plus:* Investment in other assets required	______
4. *Minus:* Avoidable costs (repairs and remodeling)	______
5. *Minus:* Net cash proceeds after tax adjustment for sale of properties retired as a result of investment	______
6. *Minus:* Investment credit (if applicable)	______
7. Total investment (sum of 1–6)	______

Cost Benefit (Annual Basis)	A. Present or Competitive	B. Your Proposal	C. ± Difference
8. Sales revenue (may be zero)	$____	$____	$____
9. *Minus:* Variable costs:			
10. Labor (including fringe benefits)	____	____	____
11. Materials	____	____	____
12. Maintenance	____	____	____
13. Other variable costs	____		____
14. Total variable costs (10–13)	____	____	____
15. Contribution margin (8–14)	____	____	____
16. *Minus:* Fixed costs:			
17. Rent or depreciation on equipment	____	____	____
18. Other fixed costs	____	____	____
19. Total fixed costs (17 + 18)	____	____	____
20. Net income before taxes (15 − 19) *	____	____	____

* If tax rate is known, calculate on after-tax basis.

Figure 3-3 (*continued*).

Accounting Rate of Return on Proposed Investment

21. Total investment cost (line 7)	$ ______
22. Average net income before taxes (line 20) *	______
23. Before-tax rate of return (line 22 ÷ line 21) †	

* If tax rate is known, calculate on after-tax basis.
† Average annual net income over life of the investment.

According to the return-on-investment approach to determining price, the reason a customer invests in a profit improvement system is to earn a superior rate of return on the funds invested in it. This puts two kinds of pressure on Profit Improvement Proposals: they must add to a customer's income or reduce a customer's costs.

Premium Price as the Conditioner of Premium Value

In Consultative Selling, premium price is not a burden. It serves as documentation of a system's value. You must aggressively promote a system's premium value of profit improvement as the validation of its price. By raising an umbrella of premium price over a system, you require customers to focus their decisionmaking on value. Instead of being defensive about price, you must use price to alert customers to expect unusual value. Price is a conditioner. It conditions you to overcome price dread and encourages an aggressive positioning of systems around added values instead of apologetically around added costs.

To use price as a conditioner to expect premium value, you must reverse the usual defensive presentation of price, which says: "My system is high-priced. *But* it delivers premium value." Instead, price should be presented as follows: "My system carries a premium price. *Therefore* you can expect premium value from it." In this way, price loses its liability. It becomes the reason why added value is obtainable as well as proof that added value is embedded in the system.

Consultative Proposing Strategies

4

How to Qualify Customer Problems

The high margins that accrue from Consultative Selling are your reward for knowing more about the customer operations you affect—and being able to improve them—than your competitors. Margins are merited by mastery of how a customer runs the business functions that are your sales targets. The more you know about them, and the better you are able to implement what you know into proposals for performing them more cost-effectively, the greater your value will be. Accordingly, the higher the price you will deserve.

Consultative Selling is industry-dedicated. Within each industry, it is function-specific. Business functions in customer companies are your end users, your true markets. According to the way they operate, they create the costs that you can reduce or do away with entirely. They can add new sales revenues or productivity if you can show them how. Your customer's business functions are the sources of the problems you will have to solve and the showcases where the value of your solutions will give testimony to your capabilities. Scoping their ways of operating should therefore be your constant preoccupation.

Remember, if you are going to sell in a consultative manner, customer business functions will be the subject matter of your consultation. The only alternative is to talk about your own processes and the products or services they produce. In that case, you will be talking to the purchasing tier, selling on a basis of competitive performance and price. Your opportunity for high margins will have vanished.

In order to know customer functions from an operating perspective and from the point of view of their financial structure, you will have to get inside customer businesses. Generic knowledge of a function based on industrywide generalizations is important and useful, but it is insufficient. Norms and averages can be extremely helpful, especially if they are used as jumping-off places to learn the specifics of individual customer operations, but by themselves they are inadequate.

The only business function profiles that customers will recognize are their own. These are also the profiles customers guard most zealously. There is good reason for this. Little perceived value comes from releasing functional operating or cost information. There are many people and organizations that can use it detrimentally, and few if any who might use it helpfully. If you want to qualify as a helpful source, you must first pay your dues—do your homework on customer businesses. Then, on the basis of what you have learned and how well you can apply it, you may be invited to propose improvements.

The ability to profile a customer business function is essential to selling at the top tier. In customer functions, you will find the problems you will propose to solve. Unless you know the nature of these problems, their importance, their financial values, and the language in which customer top management discusses them, you will be talking to yourself when you get to the top tier.

Developing a Business Function Profile

There are three ways to profile a business function that correspond with top tier management's own ways of auditing it. One is to examine its financial role within the customer's company. The second is to evaluate its operations. The third is to analyze its principal areas of intensiveness, the cost areas it depends on the most for its operations. There is a fourth way, too: study and understand a function's decision-makers.

A Function's Financial Role

Every customer operating function is a miniature business. The research and development function is a miniature science laboratory. The product engineering function is a craft workshop. The manufacturing function is a machine shop and assembly line. The sales function is a distribution organization.

Each function is tolerated by top tier management because management has decided that it is more cost-effective to own its capabilities than to buy them from the outside. They all operate at a cost. In some companies, manufacturing is expected to produce a gross margin, and sometimes the information-processing function will market portions of its database and bring in revenues. But in general, only the sales function is regularly charged with producing profits.

Because every business function is a cost center, each has the potential to run up intolerable expenses that significantly erode profits. To prevent this from happening, cost control becomes a paramount consideration. Management thinks of this mission as controlling a function's *contribution to cost.*

This is the financial context in which customer business functions exist. You must know how these functions contribute to cost or sales—that is, how many dollars they generate—inside your customer businesses as if they were your own. From the Consultative Selling point of view, they are your own: your own market.

Evaluating a Function's Operations

Business functions are processes. All processes have a flow—they have a beginning, a middle, and an end. Manufacturing begins with raw materials and ends with finished goods in inventory. Data processing begins with raw information and ends with reports. There are costs at both ends; in between, there is nothing but costs.

Every financial process has its critical few "crunch points"—the places, times, and activities where major contributions to value are made and major costs are incurred. Unless they work in the most cost-effective manner, the output from the entire process may be throttled.

Consultative sales representatives should be able to chart the flow of the key customer processes they affect. They should be able to assign appropriate costs to the most critical points that control the process—the 20 percent that contribute the 80 percent—and be able to prescribe the optimal remedy to reduce these costs or rule them out entirely.

Some of these remedies will be therapeutic; that is, they will lower an existing cost. Other remedies will be curative; they will alter a process, combine it with another, or eliminate it from the flow. In still other cases, the remedy will be to change the architecture of a process so that a completely new set of cost centers will result.

In most customer operations, workflow is cost-ineffective. It incurs unnecessary cost or it processes work ineffectively. If you can optimize it, you can improve its contribution to profit. Every dollar of cost you take out can drop to the customer's bottom line. Every improvement you make in productivity can also lower operating cost and raise the output from each dollar invested in labor, energy, and materials.

Figure 4-1 shows major business functions common to supermarkets. Any of these functions offers a consultative seller the opportunity to lower costs or raise productivity, or both.

The workflow for the packaging functions of a pharmaceuticals manufacturer is shown in Figure 4-2. Workstations A, B, and C indicate the major cost clusters that can be affected by a supplier of packaging materials: storage, materials handling and inventory, ramp productivity, and packing. If costs can be reduced or productivity increased in any of these functions, they can become consultative provinces.

A hospital laboratory's workflow is shown in Figure 4-3. The lettered workstations indicate the location of equipment used in assay testing: storage units, centrifuges, aspirators, and gamma counters. The dotted lines track the current flow of work. They show how technicians must set up for their tests, how they perform dispensing, incubation, and aspiration procedures, how they load and activate the gamma counters, and how they process their data. Every step they take requires time, adding to the laboratory's labor cost and subtracting from its productivity. Any steps that are unnecessary or repetitive incur needless cost. The dollar cost is compounded by loss of productive work time, fatigue, and an increased risk of error and waste. If the workflow can be optimized even marginally, the laboratory's contribution to hospital revenues can be significantly improved.

Analyzing a Function's Intensiveness

All customer business functions are intensive in their use of one or more resources. The sales function is labor-intensive. Research and development is technology-intensive as well as labor-intensive at an extremely costly and highly educated level of labor. Manufacturing may be energy-intensive. Plant construction and equipment modernization are capital-intensive.

The areas in which a function is intensive define the type and volume of its cost configuration. They therefore set the targets for consultative sales. If a process you affect is labor-intensive, you will want to focus your sales on reducing the amount of labor required, improving training so that lower-cost, lower-skilled labor may be substituted, replacing labor with technology, substituting external contract labor for internal workforces, or improving productivity so that each worker can increase the contribution to profit for each dollar of wages.

Figure 4-1. Supermarket business functions.

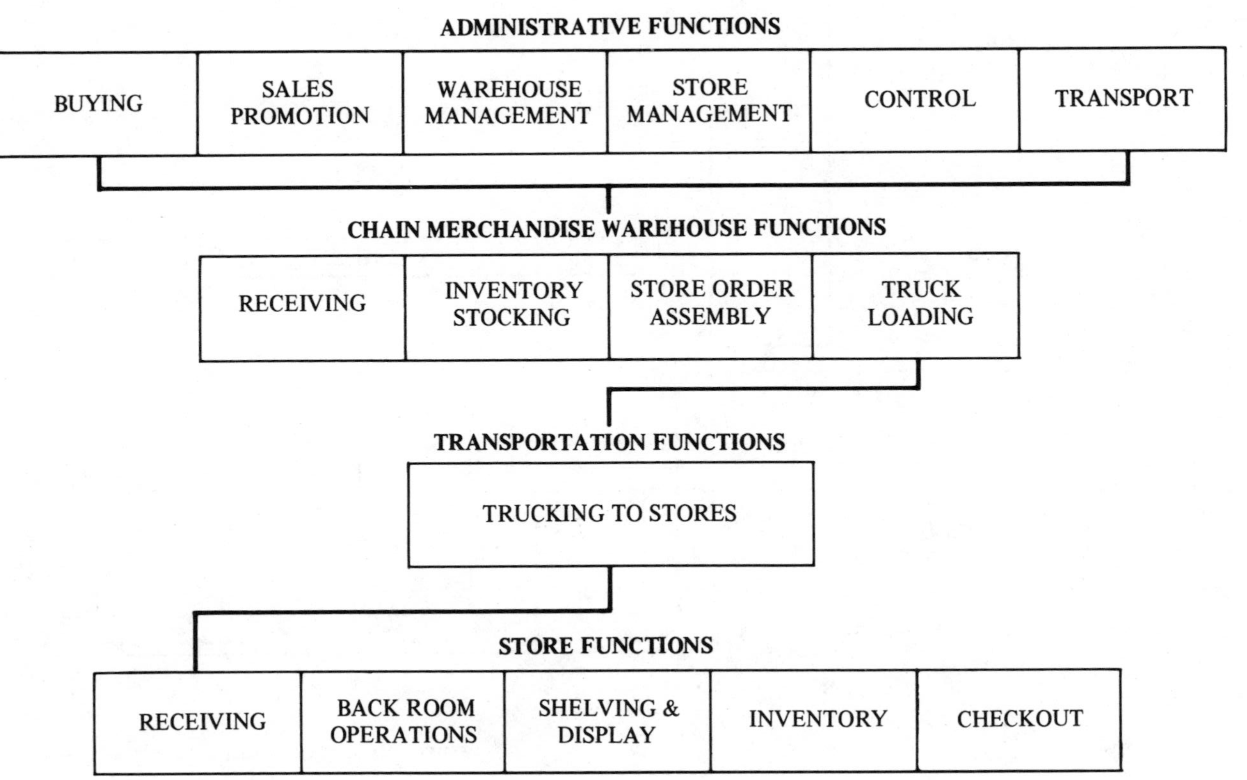

Figure 4-2. Packaging function workflow.

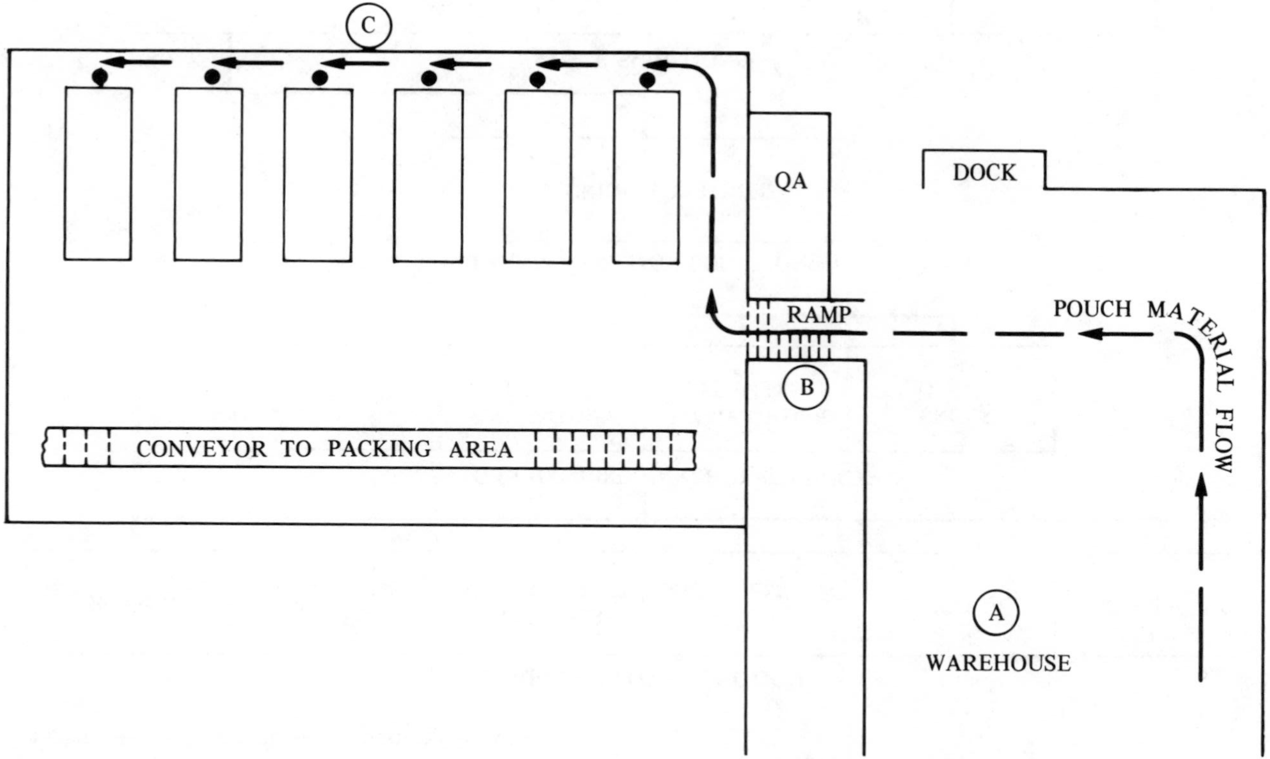

Figure 4-3. Hospital laboratory workflow.

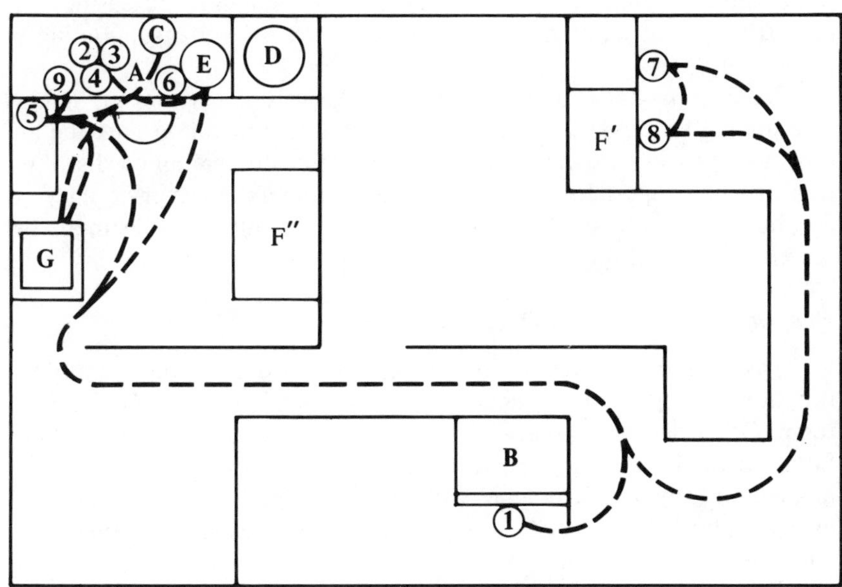

EQUIPMENT	WORKFLOW
A WORK STATION	① RECEIVE RIA KIT
B COLD STORAGE UNIT	② SET UP WORK STATION
C LAB LINE VORTEX UNIT	③ DISPENSE REAGENT
D DAMON CENTRIFUGE	④ SHAKE TUBES
E CHEMETON ASPIRATOR	⑤ INCUBATION
F′ PICKER GAMMA COUNTER	⑥ ASPIRATION
F″ BAIRD GAMMA COUNTER	⑦ LOAD GAMMA COUNTER/SET UP
G SINK	⑧ ACTIVATE GAMMA COUNTER
	⑨ PROCESS DATA

In dealing with technology intensiveness, newer forms of science such as electronic controls may contribute more cost-effectiveness than electromechanical controls. On the other hand, increasing the intensiveness of labor may be more cost-effective than upgrading a technology.

Your consultative expertise will necessarily fall within the intensive areas of your key customer business functions. You must be an assembly process expert for labor-intensive customers and a distribution process expert for sales-intensive customers. In everything you do, however, you must be expert in either reducing investment or increasing its ability to generate return.

Evaluating a Function's Decisionmakers

Decisionmakers preside over every business function, usually as function managers. Influencers reinforce decisions or argue against them. Other decisionmakers may be found at key steps in the process. Some of them are functionaries; they make a process go. Others are managers; they watch over its costs and productivity. These are the primary players you must take into consideration when you profile a customer's business function.

Primary players directly affect a function. Outside their circle are the secondary players who are affected by their decisions. These may be primary players in other functions. Taken together, they represent the deciding voices in the acceptance or rejection of your proposals.

You cannot claim to know a customer's business unless you know the decisionmakers and where they set their minimum thresholds for making affirmative buying recommendations. How much improved profit meets each decider's minimum criteria? How quickly must it start flowing in order to be regarded as soon enough? How certain must it be? How much proof is required to be convincing? What kinds of proof are most meaningful?

Only when you know these things about key customer decisionmakers can you work with them in a consultative manner. Only then can you deal with them on a businesslike basis, as opposed to simply a buyer-seller relationship. Knowing decisionmakers means knowing what is decisive for them when it comes time to invest their limited funds with you.

Scoping the Options

When you make your initial penetration of targeted customer operations, you already know a good deal about the business functions into which you sell. Even if you have only been vending, you have learned about at least three major subjects. In terms of products and services, you probably understand what has already been done by customers to make their functions more cost-effective. You know what they have purchased, from whom, for how much, and with what results. You also probably know what other companies in your customer's industry have done to solve similar problems. Some of them may be your customers too; others may be prospects. From whom have they bought? For what performance benefits? Third, you undoubtedly know something about upcoming new products and services that might create a difference in customer operations.

Just by being in business, you know most of these things. But as a consultative seller, you must know more. From the outset, you must know the options available for improved customer profit. You will have to study customer business functions so that you can prescribe the optimal mix of cost-reducing options and value-adding options for each one of their main problems.

1. *Cost-reducing options*. When you screen a business function, you must be able to learn its costs on a before-and-after basis. What are its costs right now, today? You must then be able to prescribe the best mix of available options that can accomplish some or all of three objectives. They must leave a customer with fewer dollars in costs. They must take a shorter time to reduce costs than other options. And they must be highly certain to perform.

2. *Revenue-adding options*. At the same time you screen a customer business for its costs, you should also profile the options for adding new dollar values. How can revenue-generating operations be strengthened? By how much? How can productivity be magnified? By how much, and at what dollar value? Here again, you must be able to prescribe the best available mix of options that can accomplish these improvements. They must bring a customer more money. They must bring it in more quickly than other improvements. And they must be highly certain to perform.

There is no such thing as the universal solution. No one option will fit all customers, even if the function being penetrated is the same throughout an industry. The closest you can come to broadscale generalizations are these:

1. If you can combine more value at less cost, you have the ideal solution.
2. If you can provide more value even at more cost, you may also have an ideal solution as long as the added value sufficiently exceeds the added cost.

Either of these options represents a Consultative Selling strategy. You should have them in mind as you approach a customer business with the objective of learning its costs or its ability to generate revenues. By knowing what your options are, you will be better able to select the most relevant profit improvement recommendations.

Profiling a Target Function

To vend, you need to know your own costs. To sell in a consultative manner, you need to know customer costs. To vend, you need to know your own sales opportunities. To sell as a consultant, you need to know customer sales opportunities. Realizing that you must come up with a cost-reducing or revenue-adding option, how can you learn a customer's current costs in the business functions that are important to you? How can you get a fix on the customer's unachieved sales potential? In profiling customer functions, how can you quantify with reasonable accuracy the problems and opportunities that will form the base of your penetration plans?

You will need to develop three databases, storehouses of information that will become the basic resources for top tier selling to key accounts:

1. An *industry database* on each of the industries in which you serve key customers.
2. A *customer database* on each key account customer you serve in an industry.
3. A *customer's customer database* on your key accounts' key accounts.

From your industry database, you will learn average costs, average profits on sales, average inventories and receivables, and other industry norms. The information in each of your key customer databases will allow you to compare customer performance against industry averages. In categories where a customer falls below the norms, you may find sales opportunity.

Your individual customer databases will teach you the concentration and distribution of customer costs. Where do they bunch up? Are these the same places for the industry as a whole? How heavy are they? What are their trends? Are they rising or are they coming under control? What variable factors affect them most significantly?

Your customer databases will also provide you with knowledge of where potential new sales opportunities for a customer may be found. These may include existing products, new products, combined products, new or enhanced services, superproducts, or systems. How can your customers sell more? How can they sell at higher prices? How can they extend sales into closely adjacent markets? How can they invade new markets that offer superior profit opportunity? How can they anticipate or turn back a competitive thrust?

In order for you to know your customers' business, you must know more than the performance and cost characteristics of the internal business functions that you can affect. You must also know the markets your customers sell to. They are your customers' opportunity. Their needs cause many customer business functions to operate the way they do: to manufacture the kinds of products they make, to advertise and sell the way they do, to communicate inside and outside their businesses with the telecommunications and data processing technologies they use. Only when you know your customers' customers can you understand the complete spectrum of the consultative relationship that will be available to you, the full range of costs that can be reduced and sales opportunities that can be enlarged.

The essential elements of information you will need to know about your customers' customers are exactly the same as the data you must develop on your customers themselves. You will have to learn the major cost areas your customers affect in their own key account businesses and the main sales opportunities they help them achieve.

The joint development of information is one of the strongest bonds for partnering. Shared discovery is an alliance of adventurers, each adding new values to the other. Joint research can also be cost sharing, another partnering act. At best, your key customers will realize that they will have to expand their knowledge of their own customers if they are going to be able to help them improve profits. They will, of course, also be able to use customer knowledge to sell consultatively themselves. At worst, you may have to suggest a cooperative starter survey to demonstrate the value of market knowledge.

Learning from Industry Sources

Getting into the cost structure of an industry and its customers is a three-stage effort. Setting up your databases is a front-end-loaded undertaking. After that, it is simple and inexpensive to keep them up to date. The first stage is to learn as much as you can from the multiple sources that are always available without going to your customers themselves. Then, when you take on the second and third stages that deal specifically with your accounts, you will have two advantages: you will already know a great amount, so you will have less to ask of customers, and you will have a meaningful framework on which to hang the information they share with you.

In addition to the ubiquitous publications and knowledgeable career professionals of the United States government—especially the Department of Commerce—six additional sources can help you learn the costs and revenue potentials of customers in a key industry.

1. *The people and information resources inside your own company* are the first and most obvious source. Some of your people may have been recruited from customer industries; some may even have worked for key customers. Others may have participated in market research studies that produced information relevant to your consultative needs. If your company maintains a library, its periodicals and publications can be culled for data, especially the trade magazines of your key customer industries. Your librarian can be a valuable aide in obtaining published information of all types.

2. *Trade associations* in your customer industries are staffed by people who usually devote their lifetimes to their trade. They know many generalities and often specific information about individual companies. They know the main leaders in the industry and can introduce you. Their associations also maintain industry libraries and computerized databases.

3. *Securities analysts* are professional researchers employed by brokerage houses to follow specific industries. They publish updated industry analyses that evaluate growth potential, highlight the major factors that determine profits and costs, and define trends that can forecast opportunities. Many analysts will provide personal counsel on a quid pro quo basis.

4. *Industry experts and consultants* can be retained on a one-shot or periodic basis to lay down a foundation for understanding an industry's processes and their cost structure. They can also be helpful in estimating the impact of your technology on customer costs and productivity, keeping in touch with competitive technologies, and exchanging information on industrywide business function problems and the solutions currently being implemented.

5. *Other suppliers* who sell noncompetitive products and services to the same decisionmakers at your key accounts may be willing to share their acquired knowledge of customer process costs and sales opportunities. They will probably approach the knowledge you seek

from the bias of their own interests, making their information peripheral to your needs, but nonetheless valuable.

6. *Noncustomer companies or non-key accounts* in the same industry are sometimes easier to approach for general information than your own customers. They operate the same business functions. Their costs tend to cluster at the same critical few crunch points. The potential sales opportunities affect their marketing strategies in the same way.

Learning from Public Sources

After you have done homework with multiple industry information sources and before you approach your key customers themselves, there is an important intermediate step. Every customer company reveals publicly many facts about its existing operations and plans for forthcoming investments or divestitures. These revelations are invaluable because they are authentic; they come from the horse's mouth. You should unfailingly investigate them, not only as you start up your learning curve in the transition to top tier selling but on a continuing basis. There are two major sources from which you can learn what customer companies are proclaiming or complaining about themselves:

1. *Annual reports and 10-K reports* give information on your customers' current financial condition and its trends, their objectives and the major constraints they are encountering in achieving them, how and where they are introducing new technologies and systems to alter operations that are cost-intensive, ways and areas where productivity improvement is important, new product developments and the changes they may make in the market share configurations of existing products. This information is presented to shareholders in the annual report. The 10-K version is far more detailed and far less promotional, since it is put together for the Securities and Exchange Commission.

2. *Presidential speech transcripts* are reprinted in the *Wall Street Transcript*. Chief executive officers are often interviewed by *Forbes, Business Week, Fortune,* and other business media. CEOs are increasingly appearing for interviews on network and cable television. The interview format creates a wide-ranging agenda, sometimes eliciting off-the-cuff remarks and spontaneous declarations that can yield important insights. They will also provide useful conversational tidbits when you sit down with your customer decisionmakers in the third stage of your information gathering.

Learning from Customer Sources

When you have learned as much as you can from industry sources and from sources that key customers make public, then and only then are you ready to confront your customers themselves. By this time, you will have less to ask. You will be able to phrase your inquiries in customer language, the jargon of each industry. You will be able to initiate discussion by recapitulating what you already know instead of asking for help up front. You will have shown commitment to your customer businesses by your willingness to invest homework time and effort in advance of a payback. And in the course of your studies, you will get many ideas for improving customer profit that will provoke further information from customer decisionmakers as you introduce them into your negotiations.

No information source on a customer's business can equal the customer's people themselves. They speak with authority, for two reasons. They have the inside track on customer operations; indeed, they originate much of the information themselves. Second, they believe the information is gospel. Right or wrong, their "facts" are the only real facts. Their numbers are the only hard numbers. Their costs are the costs you will have to work with. Their unfulfilled opportunities are the opportunities you will have to help them seize.

In an ideal world, customer facts and figures would be open for your asking. Every now and then it happens in exactly this way. A vendor supplier sits down once in a lifetime before the top tier managers of a key account customer and presents generalized narrative benefits of working together in a two-tier manner. For the work they will do at the top tier, the supplier proposes a partnership based on Consultative Selling strategies. The supplier reveals minimal customer knowledge and asks to be provided with the rest. The customer somehow senses the value of the benefits, and agrees.

This is called the Phil Smith approach, in honor of the first man known to have successfully accomplished it the first and only time he tried it.

The other approach is called Consultative Selling, because it is the strategy that almost always must be used. It is also known as the hard way. It is the cookbook strategy, because customers do not give internal operating information and its financial implication to vendors, especially to vendor sales representatives. As a result, a vicious circle is set up. A vendor needs inside customer information to switch from vending to top tier consultation. Yet customers do not release inside information to vendors. Without the information, a vendor will forever remain a vendor. How can the circle be broken?

Experience has shown that the only workable way is for vendors to first learn as much as possible from industry and public customer sources about customer cost problems and sales opportunities. Then they can adopt a halfway step between vending and consulting, taking on a quasi-consultative role: they share the data they have, offer tentative proposals based on their implications, and thereby motivate their customers to share the rest of what they need to know in order to achieve the proposed profits.

In this twilight zone between vending and consulting, vendors are not asking customers to give them information. They are inviting customers to trade information with them the way consultants do with their clients. Trading is acceptable to a customer, where giving is not, because trading is rewarded on the spot with a return of equal or greater value.

To make the quasi-consultative approach work on initial customer profiling, several requirements must be rigidly adhered to:

1. *You must bring something to the party;* you cannot come empty-handed. Your knowledge of a customer's industry and business must show evidence of diligence and intelligence. Your tentative suggestions for proposals to improve customer profits should demonstrate an appreciation of the customer's priorities. What is his rank order of problems? Where will the greatest rewards come from? The quickest rewards? The most certain?

The differences between the vendor's "Let me show you our new product" and the profit-improver's "Let me show you your new profits" is the difference between the euphemistically named "professional selling skills" and Consultative Selling. Vendors speak in comparatives against their competitors. The offerings they bring to the party are said to be faster, stronger, lighter—and, of course, cheaper. Consultants also speak in comparatives. But they compare a customer's costs or sales on a before-and-after basis: before they have applied the profit improvement strategies they offer, and after, as a result of applying them.

The vendor's problem is how to sell product. To solve it, vendors bring product samples. The consultant's problem is how to improve customer profits. To learn how, consultants always bring samples of profit improvement from their databases. "Let's take a look at your product line A," the consultant says. "We'll see that it is being subsidized by your profits from lines B and C. All three lines are suffering. If you could increase A's contribution by as little as one percentage point, it would break even this year and begin to carry its own weight. What if we were to reduce its manufacturing burden by $100,000? That would bring you to breakeven within the year.

"Let's take a look at this market segment of yours over here. These clients have been buying less and less from you every year. That's because their own markets have been stagnant. What if we could help them improve penetration by as little as 3 to 5 percent over the next 12 months—a profit improvement for you of at least $500,000?"

2. *You must be careful not to bend generalizations* to fit an individual customer's situation. Industry averages are useful as points of comparison with a customer's performance, but they should never be used as if they represent the customer's performance. Norms from other industries or even from other companies are not, as any customer will tell you, your customer's norms.

3. *You must be devastatingly honest* about what you have not been able to learn and therefore do not know about a customer's business. When you construct a tentative proposal, you can leave these areas blank or insert admittedly assumed cost figures. If you use assumptions, you should start with your best estimate of what a true figure would be. Then you should deliberately overestimate each customer cost item and deliberately underestimate the value of your solutions.

4. *You must be able to show dollar benefits* that meet the customer's threshold of what is significant. Unless you can do this, customers will have no incentive to trade information with you. Partnering must promise a clear reward. The customer must believe it to be achievable by working together, and must also be able to visualize continuing to receive ongoing value after the first success.

5. *You must make it simple* for a customer to agree to trade business knowledge with you. This means that you should require as little information as possible. It also means that you should not ask for any information that a customer knows is publicly available. You should not ask for major allocations of customer resources to further your work together. Your partnering requests should involve the least possible customer staff time and expense.

6. *You must believe mightily in what you propose*. Your conviction will be contagious. It will be tested by customer decisionmakers who have never before worked with you—or with any supplier—in a consultative manner. Their comfort level in going ahead will be re-

inforced by the assurance you convey and the degree of support you are willing to commit.

Asking for Rights Before Proving Rewards

The quasi-consultative approach proposes a probable reward, shows the size of the up-front investment needed, and asks for a customer contribution of knowledge to firm up the exact dimensions of the reward. Sometimes vendors try a shortcut. They lack the unique human resources to create a consultative partnership from a standing start along the lines of the Phil Smith approach. They also lack the dedication to do sufficient homework. Their approach is to ask customers for the right to study their businesses on the chance that ways and means of improving profits will be found.

Regardless of how customers respond to this approach—and occasionally they react with favor, especially smaller companies that have not had their operations already studied to a fare-thee-well—it demeans suppliers. It depositions them from any pretension of being consultative. It fixes them at the level of graduate students performing summer internships.

There are two principal risks to asking for the right to make a study before proving or even suggesting a reward. One is that studies that begin from ground zero range unnecessarily wide in search of targets. This involves many customer people, interrupting their work and increasing the chance that more than a few of them will be inconvenienced or antagonized. Some may refuse to participate. Others may think the approach is naive. These are frequently the same people who will have to be engaged in partnership if a consultative relationship is eventually established. It is not likely they will readily perceive the vendor as an equal.

The second risk is that even good results from such studies will be downgraded by the customers' top management tier. The most typical criticism is, "All they told us is what we told them." Since customers know they have provided all the information that goes into such a study, they regard the database that results as their possession. There is no felt need to reward the vendor by sharing what customers believe they have done for the vendor—rather than the other way around.

Asking for the right to study a customer's operations should be a last resort. It should never be a strategy of first choice. When a study is undertaken, it should be minimally disruptive and tightly managed for limited objectives to supplement what is already known. It should be extremely short and should never exceed its allotted time.

Managing Business Function Knowledge

Your expertise in customer business functions will emerge in this type of sequence:

1. You will know a little about one operation in one customer company in one industry.
2. You will know a lot about that one operation in that customer company.
3. You will know a little about another operation in the same customer company, as you will be invited to migrate your profit improvement strategy to another aspect of the same business function or to another function.
4. You will know a little about the same operation in a second customer company, as you penetrate other key accounts in the same industry.
5. You will know a lot about that same operation in several customer companies. You will be storing their facts and figures in your databases. Your reputation for expertise in bringing profit improvement to the operation will spread throughout the industry. The profits you bring will become the industry standard.
6. You will acquire similar databases and expertise for improving the profit contribution of other operations in the same business function and in other business functions in the industry.
7. You will extend your knowledge and repute to other closely related industries.

This is the capsule history of how major corporations have managed their customer knowledge, extending it from operation to operation within a business function, then to other business functions, then to other customer companies in the same industry, and then to other industries. In order to grow their key account sales at high margins, they have marketed their knowledge of customer business problems and opportunities. On the surface, they have been selling profit-improving solutions. But the underlying value has been their understanding of customer problems. They appear as solution experts. At rock bottom, however, they are process-smart, operations-smart, function-smart—that is, customer-smart. Only then can they be smart suppliers.

As you learn how to manage customer knowledge resources, you will discover two truths. No customer wants to be first with anything new. Yet as soon as something new produces superior results, every customer wants to possess it on an exclusive basis. These paradoxical attitudes will be encountered as you take the first steps from vending to Consultative Selling. Finding the first customer to work with, to let you get inside heretofore proprietary operations, will be more difficult than finding the second. Yet working with a second customer in the same industry may also be difficult because the first customer will want to monopolize your function-profiling skills and profit-improving strategies.

In spite of these initial constraints, you will know that you have achieved consultant recognition in a customer industry when a remarkable event occurs. You will be *invited* by customers to profile their business functions—not to bid on their business but to study its cost structure and its sales opportunity. At that point, your knowledge of industry norms will come importantly into play. Once you have captured the knowledge of their functions, your proposals for profit improvement will follow naturally. After all, who will be better equipped?

What you know about customer functions will not be what you sell. But what you sell will always be based on what you know.

In many sales organizations, realization is accompanied by pain, as the balance of power swings from products and pricing specialists to customer operations and applications specialists. Product knowledge will always be preeminent at the vendor's purchasing tier. But a sales organization will be permanently welded into position there until it acquires the customer data that enable it to move up. The short-run agonies of change must be balanced against the long-term agonies of decreasing margins, increasing competitive parity, and rising costs that can never be retrieved by price. The difference between being able to obtain top margins at the top tier and suffering eroding margins at the purchasing tier is the value added by Consultative Selling.

5

How to Quantify Your Solution

Customer profit improvement begins with knowledge of how customers make the profits that you are going to improve: how they make their money right now. This is the starting point for Consultative Selling. Unless Consultative Selling strategies can improve the profits a customer can make, the customer will not be a prospect for high-margin sales.

Knowledge of how customers make profit starts with their own records of performance. For public companies, these are the balance sheet and the income statement. Privately held companies must be assessed by speculation, with the best clues obtained from comparison with public companies in the same industry.

Proposal Background from the Customer's Balance Sheet

A balance sheet is a snapshot of a business that shows its financial condition at the moment in time when it is snapped. If you learn how to read it, you can picture the financial structure of a customer's business, and this will be very useful in helping you spot your best opportunities for profit improvement.

Balance sheets can take many forms, and the items that appear on them may vary according to the character of each business and its particular circumstances. A conventional balance sheet appears in Figure 5-1. It contains five sections. Two appear on the left-hand, or asset,

Figure 5-1. Balance sheet expressed as a statement of assets and liabilities.

BALANCE SHEET	
ASSETS	LIABILITIES
Current Assets	Current Liabilities
	Long-Term Liabilities
Fixed Assets	Capital (Capital Stock and Retained Earnings)

side of the statement: current assets and fixed assets. On the right-hand side are current liabilities, long-term liabilities, and capital. When the dollar values assigned to the items on each side are totaled, a balance sheet must balance. Components of the balance sheet's five elements are as follows:

1. *Current assets.* Cash as well as receivables and inventories that are expected to be liquidated into cash within one year.
2. *Fixed assets.* The land, buildings, and equipment used in the operation of the business.
3. *Current liabilities.* Accounts payable, short-term bank loans, current installments of long-term loans, bonds or mortgages payable, accrued payroll due to employees, accrued taxes, and other amounts due to third parties within one year.
4. *Long-term liabilities.* Bonds, mortgages payable, and other loans due beyond one year.
5. *Capital.* The value of a business to its owners; also called equity. It is created either by direct investment of funds in the

> business or by profits that are retained after payment of dividends to owners or stockholders. Since equity is determined by subtracting liabilities from assets, both sides of the balance sheet will balance.

To understand the character of the underlying funds, you must translate the customer balance sheet into the form shown in Figure 5-2. In effect, 5-2 is an X-ray of 5-1.

The left-hand side of Figure 5-2 represents the funds invested in the business operations of a customer. It shows at a particular point in time where and in what form these funds reside. Current assets are the funds invested in the circulating capital of the business. Funds invested in the facilities used to operate the business are fixed assets.

The right-hand side of Figure 5-2 shows the current sources of the funds that have been invested. From it, we can determine the specific proportion of the customer's total invested funds that has been contributed by vendors and banks on a short-term basis; by banks, insurance companies, and bondholders on a long-term basis; and by the owners

Figure 5-2. Balance sheet expressed as a statement of funds invested and sources of funds.

<table>
<tr><th colspan="2">BALANCE SHEET</th></tr>
<tr><th>FUNDS INVESTED</th><th>SOURCES OF FUNDS</th></tr>
<tr><td rowspan="2">Circulating Capital</td><td>Vendors
Banks
(Short-term)</td></tr>
<tr><td rowspan="2">Banks
Insurance Companies
Bondholders
(Long-term)</td></tr>
<tr><td rowspan="2">Facilities</td></tr>
<tr><td>Stockholders</td></tr>
</table>

and stockholders as a result of direct investment or retained operating profits.

As a rule, management of the left-hand side of the balance sheet, representing the funds invested in a customer's operations, is the responsibility of operating management. The right-hand side of the balance sheet, representing the sources of funds, is the responsibility of financial management. Since the cost of acquiring and maintaining funds differs depending on their source, money management is an important function contributing to profitability.

Consultative sales representatives who deal in products and services related to money management—financial systems, for example—will want to pay particular attention to the right-hand side of the balance sheet. Examining competitive sources of funds may be useful in determining how their products or services can reduce the customer's cost of acquisition or maintenance of funds and thereby contribute to profit. On the other hand, consultants whose products or services affect the operations of the customer's business—computerized design and manufacturing systems, for example—will be more interested in the funds invested in operating assets. Because credit terms affect the financial management function, they will be of interest to all consultants regardless of the products or services they sell.

Proposal Background from the Customer's Income Statement

Increases or decreases in the value of a customer company's capital are generally the result of one or more of three conditions:

1. Capital value will increase if additional capital is obtained.
2. Capital value will decrease if dividends are paid out.
3. Capital value will increase if the net result of operations is a profit and will decrease if the net result of operations is a loss.

By far the most significant factor in determining capital value is the net result of operations or the earning power of the business. This aspect of profitmaking is reported in a separate document known as the income statement or profit and loss (P&L) statement. On it, profit appears as the remainder of revenues after expenses have been subtracted. This statement of profit on the bottom line is the benchmark from which your profit improvement objectives must take off. How much better can you do than the customer is already doing? Every dollar you can add represents incremental gain for the customer and provides the basis of incremental price for you.

The P&L statement also shows you where a customer's money goes—where investment is most intensive and where any reduction will be welcome. A typical dealership or distributor will state its intensiveness like this:

	($000)
Materials	850
Labor	1,500
Overhead	900

You may not be able to reduce fixed assets, at least not in the short term. But labor and materials costs are prime targets for cost reduction proposals.

The Circulating Capital Principle

Profit is made by the circulation of business capital. Every business is founded on capital, or funds that start in the form of cash. The objective of business is to make that initial cash grow into more cash. The way this is accomplished is to circulate the capital, the initial cash, through three transfer points. Each transfer adds value:

1. The initial cash circulates first into *inventories*.
2. Then the inventories circulate into *receivables*.
3. The receivables finally circulate back into *cash*, completing one cycle.

This three-step process demonstrates the principle of circulating capital. Every business depends on it for its income.

Circulating capital is the current assets of a business. They go to work in profitmaking as soon as cash is invested in accumulating inventories. Every time raw materials are purchased or processed, inventories come into existence. Another name for production scheduling could really be inventory conversion. Manufacturing adds further to the values of inventories, and so do all the other processing functions of a business that transfer value from cash to product costs on a dollar-for-dollar basis.

Figure 5-3 shows the profitmaking process that occurs as capital

Figure 5-3. Profitmaking through capital circulation.

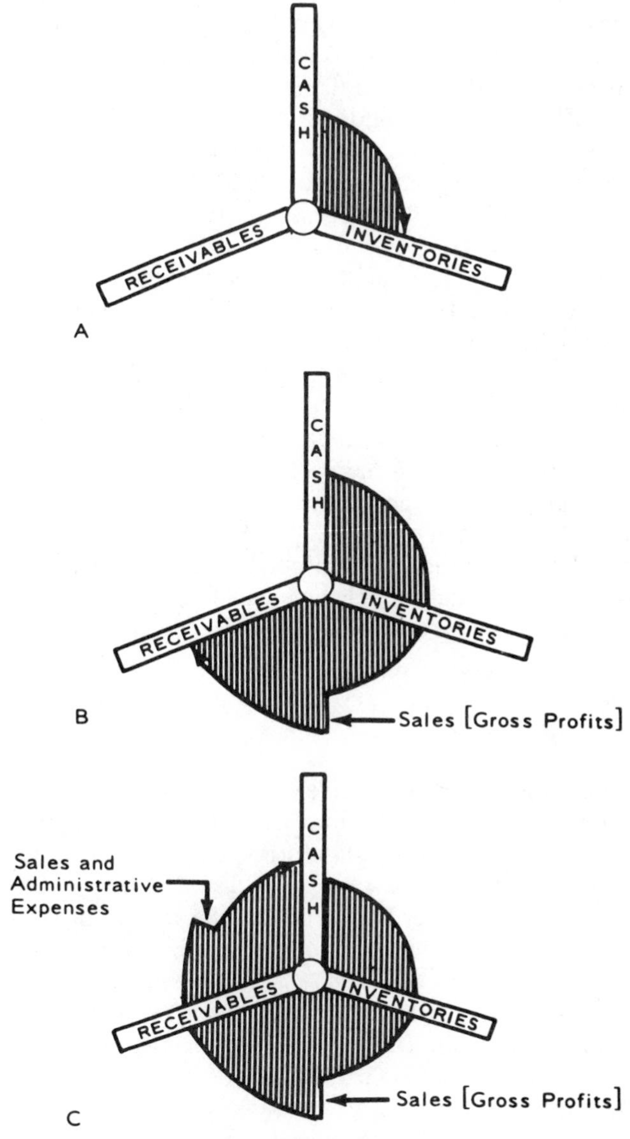

funds circulate through a customer's business. At A the funds are in the form of cash. As the business operates, the funds change form. The initial cash is transferred into inventories, as raw materials are purchased, labor is paid, and finished goods are manufactured and sometimes transported from plant to warehouse.

When sales occur at B, funds flow from inventories—the manufactured goods—into receivables. As they flow, the magnitude of the funds increases since inventories are valued at cost and receivables are valued at selling price. This increase represents the gross profit on sales. The greater the gross profit rate, the greater the increase in funds during each rotation of the capital circulation cycle.

At C, the funds earned by the collection of receivables flow back once again into cash. Before they do, they are reduced by the sales and administrative expenses that have been disbursed throughout the operating cycle.

At this point, one full cycle of capital circulation has been completed. It has resulted in an increase in the number of dollars in the circulating capital fund. This increase is the difference between gross profits and selling/administration expenses. In other words, a profit is made when the circulating capital of the business turns over one cycle. The more cycles through which you can help turn your customer's circulating capital during an operating year, the greater the profit the customer can earn. This is the principle of *turnover*.

The Turnover Principle

The circulation of capital funds in a customer's business takes on meaning only when it relates to time. Since capital funds turn over in a complete cycle from cash to inventories, then to receivables, and finally back into cash again, their rate of flow can be measured as the rate of turnover. The faster the turnover, the greater the profit.

Stepping up a customer's turnover rate through profit improvement is the consultative sales representative's most important function. Unless your profit projects are by and large directed to improving the turnover of the capital employed in your customer's business—especially the capital that is in the form of inventories—you cannot accomplish your mission.

Turnover will generally offer more opportunities than any other strategy for profit improvement. The most common way to improve turnover rate is through increased sales volume and lowered operating fund requirements. In some situations, turnover may be improved by decreasing sales or even increasing the investment in operating assets.

You are in excellent position to help improve a customer's turn of circulating capital since, as Figure 5-4 shows, the drive wheel that rotates capital is sales. You must continually search for the optimal relationship between your customer's sales volume and the investment in operating funds required to achieve it. At the point where the optimal relationship exists, the turnover rate will yield the best profit.

In Figure 5-4, the circumference of the sales wheel represents $200,000 worth of sales during a 12-month operating period. The sales wheel drives a smaller wheel representing circulating capital. The circumference of the circulating wheel equals the amount of dollars invested in working funds, in this case $100,000. Enclosing the circulating capital wheel is a larger wheel, also driven by sales, that represents the total capital employed. It includes the circulating capital of $100,000 plus another $100,000 invested in plant and facilities. Thus the circumference of the wheel representing total capital employed is $200,000, equal to the sales drive wheel.

When annual sales are $200,000 and total capital employed in the operation is $200,000, the annual turnover rate of total funds invested is 100 percent, or one turn per year. The portion of the total that is circulating capital, amounting to $100,000, will turn over at the rate of 200 percent, or twice a year.

Each of the three elements of circulating capital—cash, receivables, and inventories—will have its own individual turnover rate. Inventory turnover is calculated according to the number of months' supply on hand. A six months' supply would represent two turns per year, or a 200 percent annual turnover rate. Turnover of receivables is expressed as the number of days' business outstanding. If 90 days of business are outstanding, the receivables turnover is four turns per year, or 400 percent.

Since circulating capital increases every time it completes one turn, your job is to find ways to increase customer turnover through the use of your product and service systems. You can exercise two options for improving turnover. One way, option A, is by increasing sales. The other way is by decreasing the amount of money invested in circulating capital, option B.

Figure 5-4 shows an opportunity to double customer sales to $400,000 per year without increasing the $200,000 of total funds employed in the business. This is option A. The turnover rate will be increased from 100 to 200 percent. At the same time, the turnover rate of circulating capital increases from 200 to 400 percent.

If the consultant cannot increase the customer's sales, option B offers an alternative opportunity to improve turnover. Even though

Figure 5-4. Turnover.

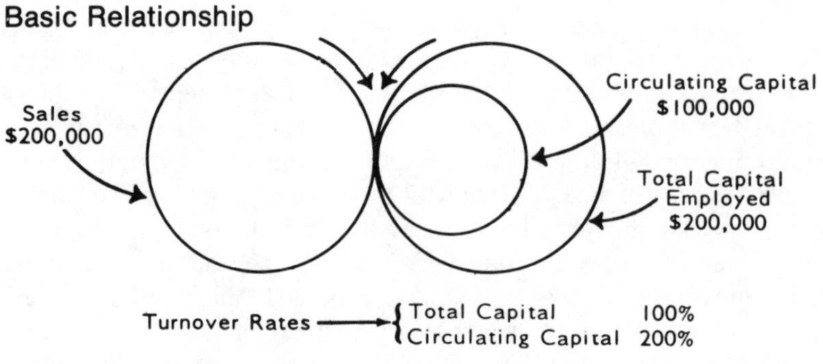

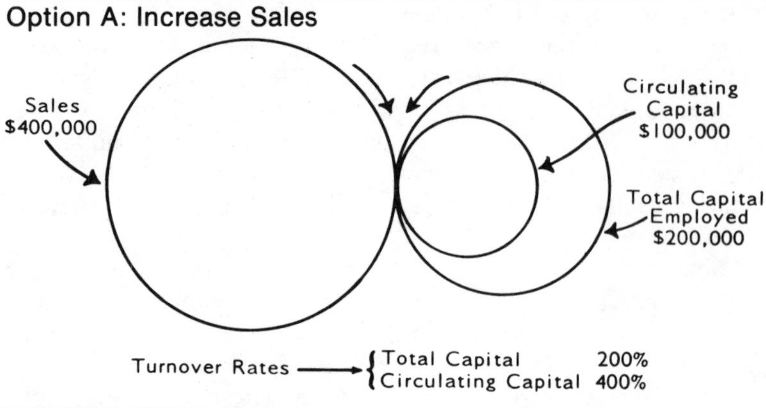

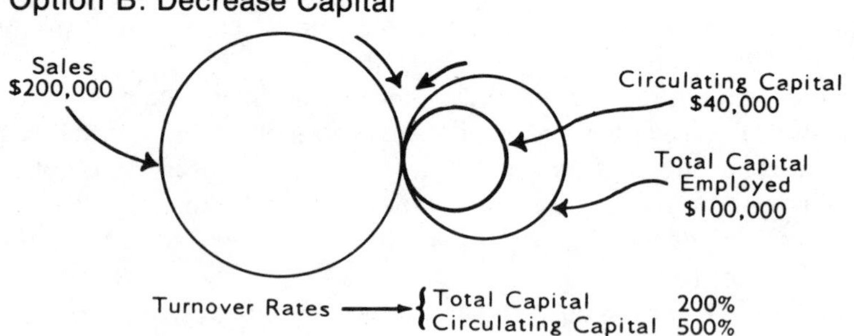

sales remain at the same annual rate of $200,000, turnover can be increased if total capital employed is reduced from $200,000 to $100,000. This includes a parallel reduction in circulating capital from $100,000 to $40,000. These reductions help the consultant improve the turnover rate of total capital employed from 100 to 200 percent and that of circulating capital from 200 to 500 percent. This strategy for improving turnover means that the operating funds of the customer's business are being worked harder.

The profit improvement created by options A and B can be readily appreciated by multiplying the increase in funds generated at each turn of the operating cycle by an increasing number of turns. If the operating profit from one turn in the basic relationship shown in Figure 5-4 is $50,000, the profit realized by option A would be doubled to $100,000. In option B, profit would remain at $50,000 but $100,000 of funds would be released from operations that could be used to generate additional business or reduce indebtedness.

Opportunities abound for improving a customer's turnover. The reason is simple. The sum total of funds employed in a customer's business represents the many individual funds that make up circulating and fixed capital. An improvement in the turnover of any one of these funds will correspondingly improve the turnover of the total funds employed. Therefore, you can zero in on any component of a customer's "turnover mix" without having to consider any of the others or their sum total. For example, improvement in the turnover of any single item in a customer's inventory—including your own product—will improve total turnover and consequently contribute to profit improvement.

Contribution Margin

The key to profits is contribution margin—how much margin each product line or business unit contributes to a customer's total profits. Affecting a customer's contribution margins is a key objective of Consultative Selling. There are two ways to do this. You can help increase sales volume at the current contribution margin. Or you can help increase contribution margin at the current volume of sales.

Figure 5-5 shows how contribution margin works. It is calculated by subtracting variable costs from sales revenues. In the example, a customer's total contribution margin is $.095. That means that each single dollar of sales is currently contributing a margin of 9.5 cents to cover the customer's fixed operating overhead of $221,000. It takes a

Figure 5-5. Analysis of profit contribution by product line. (Dollars in thousands.)

		Total	Product Lines		
			A	B	C
1. Sales	$	2,600	1,742	650	208
	%	100.0	67.0	25.0	8.0
2. Cost of Sales	$	2,106	1,440	520	146
	%	81.0	82.7	80.0	70.0
3. Gross profit (1 - 2)	$	494	302	130	62
	%	19.0	17.3	20.0	30.0
4. Wages	$	221	134	65	22
	%	8.5	7.7	10.0	10.5
5. Other	$	26	10	13	3
	%	1.0	0.6	1.9	1.5
6. Total (4 + 5)	$	247	144	78	25
	%	9.5	8.3	11.9	12.0
7. Contribution margin (3 - 6)	$	247	158	52	37
	%	9.5	9.0	8.1	18.0

lot of $1 sales to contribute enough 9.5 cents' worth of margins to cover $221,000 of overhead. Even when sales do that, the customer merely breaks even. That is where you come in. If you can increase sales or decrease the variable costs that subtract from sales revenues, you can improve customer profits.

The consultant's choices are shown in Figure 5-5. If you want to work on product line A, you can improve profits best by improving sales. While it has only a 17.3 percent gross profit, it also has a 9.0 percent contribution. Any increase in sales volume will produce new profits. On the other hand, if you work on product line B, you will have to reduce its variable costs. Its 20 percent gross profit exceeds that of A. But it is making only an 8.1 percent contribution after variable expenses. If you can reduce its expenses, you can improve its contribution even without increasing sales volume.

Measuring Profit Improvement

Customers define a problem as a cost that *can be* reduced or a sales opportunity that *can be* realized. Customers define a solution as a cost that *has been* reduced or sales revenue that *has been* gained. In either case, customer profit has been improved. The best rule of thumb for every consultant to follow is that a customer problem has been solved when the prescribed profit improvement has been produced by the consultant's system.

Customers measure their solutions according to *incremental analysis*. This is sometimes called microanalysis, since it evaluates the new profit earned by a consultant's system.

Three methods of incremental analysis are commonly used to measure a system's profit contribution: payback, discounted cash flow (DCF), and accounting rate of return (AROR).

Payback

The payback method measures profit improvement according to how long it will take to recoup the cash outlay required to obtain a system. Payback is essentially a criterion of "cash at risk." If payback can be achieved quickly, the risk factor will be low and the return will be high. If a system's benefits continue after payback, the return will be even higher.

Discounted Cash Flow

The DCF method measures profit improvement by converting the cash values of a system's costs and benefits into a present-time value. Discounted cash flow analysis is usually used in conjunction with payback analysis and the AROR approach on major systems. There are two variations of the DCF method:

1. *Net present value (NPV)* applies a predetermined interest rate to discount future cash flow in order to match it with a system's required cash outlay. The interest rate may be based on a customer's cost of capital or an arbitrary "hurdle rate" that has been set as the minimum payback for new investments. A high net present value is a customer signal to proceed.

2. *Internal rate of return (IRR)* is similar to net present value but does not contain a predetermined discount factor. The IRR is the interest rate that discounts a system's net cash flow to zero present value when compared with its required cash outlay. If the IRR rate exceeds the hurdle rate, a customer will usually proceed.

Accounting Rate of Return

The AROR method measures profit improvement by comparing the average income or expenses saved over the life of a system with the investment outlay required to obtain it. The percentage rate of return that results is based solely on the incremental income generated by the system. It reflects the earnings rate of return on the incremental investment. Many customers favor this method because it is oriented to their balance sheets and income statements even though it ignores the time value of money.

All three measurement methods have certain elements in common. They all use a basic cost-benefit analysis. All of them seek to determine the present value of a system investment on a cash basis, including the opportunity costs involved; the operating revenue; the operating costs; and the difference between operating revenue and operating costs, which equals the benefits.

The ROI Connection

Of the three methods, only the accounting rate of return relates to the return on investment, ROI, which is used to evaluate total customer company performance. This total return on investment must be narrowed down to AROR in order to evaluate an *incremental investment,* such as a specific system. A system's AROR can, therefore, be considered as the added rate of profit that the system can add to the customer's ROI.

AROR/ROI Interrelationships

The interrelationship between ROI and AROR can be seen by the similarity between their formulas:

$$\text{ROI} = \frac{\text{net profit}}{\text{sales}} \times \frac{\text{sales}}{\text{investment}}$$

$$\text{AROR} = \frac{\text{net profit}}{\text{investment}}$$

For calculating the accounting rate of return, sales are eliminated from the ROI formula. This is because total customer company analysis is not relevant for most systems investments. The impact of most systems, even huge capital-intensive systems, becomes swallowed up in a customer's total ROI. The consultant cannot identify an individual system's contribution when it is dispersed over such a broad base. Therefore, to make a system's incremental contribution measurable, its impact should be calculated according to AROR.

Net income is not the sole basis for determining AROR. Gross profit may be an appropriate measure of a system's income if no incremental operating costs are involved or if operating costs cannot be separated on incremental sales. Contribution margin may also be an appropriate measure of system income if no incremental fixed costs are incurred or if fixed costs cannot be separated.

System-Opportunity Identification

The return-on-investment approach is the best diagnostic tool to identify consultative sales opportunities. As the ROI formula shows, a consultative opportunity is always present when either a customer's operating profit rate or turnover can be improved.

Any system that a consultant recommends must meet customer standards of what constitutes an adequate return on investment. A system whose promise of profit improvement falls below this standard will probably be rejected as not being worth the investment. It will usually be ruled out by one of three standards for determining whether a given rate of return on investment is adequate: its investment exceeds the basic cost of money, its payback is too risky, or the return falls below the amount that customers believe they have the right to expect from their technological sophistication.

The Return-on-Investment Yardstick

In order to tell whether the increased sales you propose from a profit improvement project are good or poor, you will need an accurate yardstick. In many selling organizations, profit is commonly expressed as a percentage of sales price or as an absolute amount per unit. But any method of measuring profit as a percentage of sales is insufficient for consultative purposes since it takes into account only two elements of profit: sales revenues and cost. The difference between them is then calculated as a percentage of sales. Most companies call that difference profit. Profit, however, has a very important third component: *time*.

From the point of view of return, profit can be regarded as the ratio of income earned *during an operating cycle* to the amount of capital invested to produce it. Thus profits have two costs: time costs and costs of producing the product or service. When profit is compared with its funded investment, it is being expressed as a return on investment, or ROI.

Return on investment is an analytic tool that has three qualities in its favor for your purposes: (1) it is a fair measurement of profit contribution; (2) it is helpful in directing attention to the most immediate profit opportunities, allowing them to be ranked on a priority basis; and (3) it is likely to be readily understood and accepted by financial managers as well as sales and marketing managers of your customer companies.

Figure 5-6 represents the formulas for calculating return on investment. The formulas relate the major operating and financial factors required in profitmaking to the rate used to measure the profit that is made: the rate of profit per unit sales in dollars, the rate of turnover of operating funds, the funds required to finance business operations, and the total investment of capital employed, including working assets, plants, and facilities.

The customer's sole economic justification for investing in your profit improvement projects is to earn a superior rate of return on the funds invested. This truism must be interpreted in two ways. One is in terms of income gained. The other is in terms of costs avoided in obtaining investment funds, costs of retaining such funds, and costs

Figure 5-6. Return-on-investment formulas.

A. Options for Improving ROI by Improving Turnover

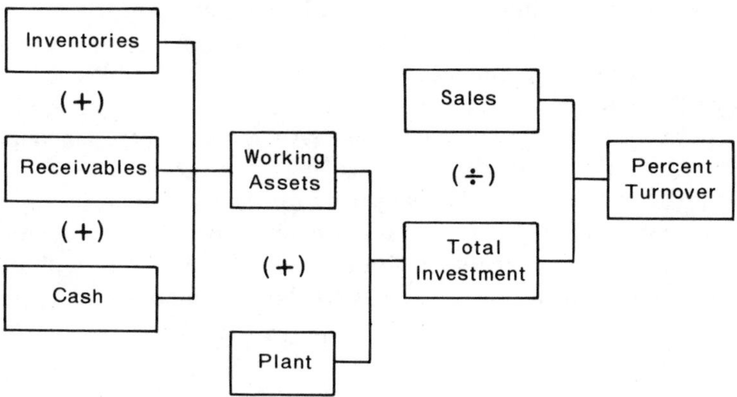

B. Options for Improving ROI by Improving Operating Profit

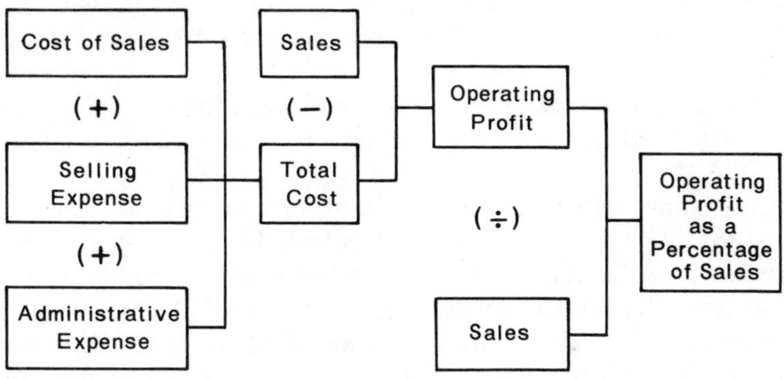

suffered by denying their use for alternative, potentially more profitable projects.

Return-on-Investment Diagnostic Techniques

Diagnosis lies at the heart of consulting. Diagnostic techniques that are based on return on investment lie at the heart of diagnosis.

As Figure 5-6 shows, ROI is the product of the rate of operating profit expressed as a percentage of sales and the rate of turnover. Any time you want to improve a customer's ROI, you must first diagnose a problem in the customer's operating rate or an opportunity in the customer's turnover.

Part A of Figure 5-6 shows the ingredients of ROI expressed as turnover. If you examine each of those ingredients, you will find profit opportunities that can improve turnover. You can, for example, recommend a project to reduce your customer's receivables. This will reduce the amount of funds invested in working assets, thus reducing the customer's total investment base. As a result, you can improve your customer's profit without increasing sales volume.

Part B of Figure 5-6 shows options for diagnosing profit improvement if your objective is to increase operating profit. You can recommend a project to lower the customer's cost of sales. This will reduce total costs and enable the customer to show an increase in operating profit.

Seeking Simple Opportunities

A consultant can find many relatively simple ways to recommend profit improvement. If you sell to supermarkets, you can show each chain's central headquarters or even individual store managers how substituting your brands for others, or increasing the number and location of their shelf facings, may improve profit per case or per $100 of sales.

Profit improvement for a manufacturing customer may lie in improving the profit of dealers and distributors. By helping a customer's distributor organization increase its contribution—something the customer cannot directly control yet must nonetheless influence—you can help your customer raise the profit on sales made through this channel.

A distributor's largest single investment is likely to be in inventory. The key to distributor inventory control is finding the minimum investment required to maintain adequate sales and service. One way of measuring the utilization of inventory investment is to compare a distributor's inventory turnover with his industry's average. Inventory turnover can be computed by using this formula:

$$\frac{\text{Cost of sales for one year}}{\text{Average inventory}} = \text{inventory turnover}$$

If a customer's distributors are in a business whose inventory turns an average of 4.5 times a year, or once every 80 to 90 days, you can help a distributor whose turnover is lower than average see the problem this way:

$$\frac{\text{Projected cost of sales}}{\text{Projected average inventory level}} = \frac{\$370{,}000}{\$100{,}000} = 3.7 \text{ Inventory turnover}$$

To help this distributor increase turnover to approach the 4.5 industry average, you will have to help the distributor reduce inventory investment. To do this, you must first find out what level of inventory investment can yield a 4.5 turnover. Divide the distributor's projected cost of sales by the desired 4.5 turnover, which results in an $82,000 inventory. It now becomes clear that you can help the distributor achieve profit improvement by reducing inventory investment by $18,000. Then you can turn your attention to optimizing the inventory mix.

The consultant's best approach to inventory reduction is usually through product-line smoothing. Distributors almost always carry too many items in their lines. An inventory burdened by too many items can cause a dissipation of the distributor's sales concentration, extra handling costs, waste through obsolescence or spoilage, and, of course, higher inventory carrying costs, higher insurance costs, and overextended investment.

To analyze a distributor's inventory, you can simply rank the products in the line according to their cost of sales and then compute their inventory turnover. Such an analysis could look like this:

> Products A, B, C, and D account for 57% of the cost of sales but only 34% of inventory. These products turn over inventory by an average of 6.2 times a year.
>
> Products E, F, G, H, J, and K account for 43% of the cost of sales but 66% of inventory. These products turn over inventory by an average of only 2.4 times a year.

The inventory turnover analysis in Figure 5-7 shows what it costs the distributor to carry inventory. By comparing the carrying costs of inventory to forecast sales volume, you can begin to learn more precisely what inventory the distributor should maintain. The first four products are apparently well controlled. They have an average turnover rate of 6.2 percent and 1 percent average carrying cost as a percentage of sales. You now know that you must concentrate on reducing inventory whose average turnover rate is only 2.4 percent and average

Figure 5-7. Inventory turnover analysis.

		INVENTORY			
Product	% of Sales	Average $	% of Average	Turn-over	Carrying Cost as % of Sales
A	15	7,000	7	8.2	0.8
B	17	9,000	9	7.0	0.9
C	14	11,000	11	4.7	1.3
D	11	7,000	7	5.8	1.1
Subtotal	57	34,000	34	6.2	1.0
All Other Products	43	66,000	66	2.4	2.6
Total	100	100,000	100	3.7	1.7

carrying cost is 2.6 as a percentage of sales. This will help bring the distributor's inventory down to the $82,000 level that should contribute to the projected 4.5 inventory turnover.

Managing a Profit Improvement Portfolio

The incremental value of a consultant's relationship with a key account customer is simple to calculate. At any given time, it is the sum total of earnings from all a consultant's Profit Improvement Proposals. A few proposals will probably be spectacularly successful. But for the most part, steady, modest success is all that is required.

Each proposal should be successful in its own right. Beyond that, it should also lead naturally into the next successful project. As your profit improvement contributions accumulate in a sausage-link chain, you will be building equity. This equity will consist of the value of the portfolio of Profit Improvement Proposals you have installed in each account. The reward for good work will be more work. By inviting you to remain in the game and try to improve profit one more time after each success, your customer is acknowledging a consultative partnership. As with all partnerships, "congratulations" is always followed by "you're vulnerable."

You, the consultant, are only as good as your last proposal. This should cause you to be financially conservative. Paradoxically, however, you will also have to be creatively daring in conceiving profit improvement opportunities and planning to capture them. The net result of combining these two characteristics becomes the essence of your personal consultative style.

In setting about to construct a profit improvement portfolio, you should start small. At the outset you must be content to make a single profit improvement in one business function or one product line in one account. Since the first proposal will probably be evaluated more critically than any of its successors, you must follow one injunction above all others: *The first time out, be successful.*

6

How to Sell the Customer's Return

The penetration plan is your annual blueprint for getting into and staying in the business of a principal customer. The way you get in is by improving the customer's profit. The way you stay in is by continuing to improve the customer's profit, extending it to the solution of new problems, and never letting go. Last year's profit-improver who has let go is last year's supplier of choice.

The databasing process for penetration planning requires answers to three critical questions that can determine up to 80 percent of your profitability on sales:

1. Who is my customer?
2. What can I do to improve my customer's profit?
3. What will my customer do for me in return?

The answer to the first question is crucial. Your customer is never a company as a whole, nor is it even a division. It is a specific business function manager within a division whose costs you can reduce or whose contribution to sales you can increase. If you are IBM, your customer is not PepsiCo. Nor is it PepsiCo's Frito-Lay division. It is the manager of Frito-Lay's inventory control function, for example, whose profit contribution you will be improving.

Similarly, if you are AT&T, your customer is not Merrill Lynch or, within it, the Diversified Financial Services division. Nor is it the division's real estate management functions. Your penetration plan may be directed to the division, but the business function manager in real estate telemarketing is your customer. It is that manager's profit contribution you will be improving. If you are Nabisco, your customer is not Grand Union supermarkets. It is the dry cereal department management group throughout the chain.

Planning to penetrate business functions within divisions or departments of customer companies is a far cry from vending commodity merchandise to purchasing managers on a price-performance basis. It is a totally different process: data-dependent rather than persuasion-dependent. Its database must therefore be structured to support the differences in sales strategy that a consultative approach demands.

High Penetration Objectives

Opportunity databasing hinges on one central concept: maximizing contribution. Two kinds of contributions are involved. One is your profit contribution to a customer. You must maximize it. The other is a customer's profit contribution to you. You must maximize that also. This defines the consultative concept of opportunity: the chance to be a maximizer of customer profits.

The role of a profit maximizer differs from the role of a needs analyst or a benefit provider or a problem-solver. All these are intermediate steps. Through needs analysis, the provision of benefits, and the solving of problems, profits become improved. This is the ultimate step. If it does not take place, all the intermediate objectives can still be accomplished, but they will be in vain.

High penetration objectives—superior profit objectives for your customer and for you as well—are financial objectives. Nothing supersedes them. They must come first in your penetration plan because they are the purpose of the plan. The only reason to plan is to be able to set and achieve high financial objectives.

The objectives of your plan should be databased in the following manner:

1. The most likely profit contribution that will be made *by you* to each customer:
   1.1 This year.
   1.2 Next year.
   1.3 Third year.
2. The most likely profit contribution that will be made *to you* by each customer:
   2.1 This year.
   2.2 Next year.
   2.3 Third year.

"Most likely" profits are a conservative estimate. They are a trifle more bullish than bearish, but only a trifle. They represent the contributions that can be expected if most strategies work according to plan and if there are no important hitches that have not been planned for. In practice, they should come out just about right.

If you help customers improve their profits from incremental sales, you will have to adjust the gross profits by the customers' effective tax rate before you commit to an objective. If you improve customer profits by cost savings that can flow directly to the bottom line, you can calculate the profits as net incremental gain. Only the net counts. Neither you nor your customers can take anything else to the bank.

The total annual contribution you expect to make to your customers will be the sum of all the Profit Improvement Proposals you plan to install in their business functions during a year. The contribution your customers will make to you will be the sum of your profits from the sale of each proposal that are collectible during the same year. Two ratios are helpful to monitor how effectively your resources are being allocated to obtain each customer's contribution. One compares profits to the expenditures required to achieve them; this is return on investment. The second is the more traditional ratio of revenues to expenses.

High Penetration Strategy

Objectives are a plan's purpose. Strategies are the methods of achieving objectives. In Consultative Selling, strategies are packaged in Profit Improvement Proposals. Each proposal represents a strategy to improve customer profit by solving a cost or sales problem. If the customer is a not-for-profit organization or a government agency, proposal strategies will focus on reducing costs and improving the dollar value of productivity. Either way, the mix of strategies must make a measurable impact on customer profit or operational performance, or both.

Profit Improvement Proposals are the sales vehicles for penetration strategies. They are designed to penetrate the customer's business at high-level points of entry. Each proposal contains a strategy for solving a specific customer problem. The sum total of proposals for the period of a year constitutes the annual top tier strategy for a customer.

There are three steps to take before you can propose profit improvement:

1. Analyze a customer's business position.
2. Position penetration strategies.
3. Pinpoint penetration opportunities.

Selling to a Customer's Business Position

A customer's business position determines your sales strategy. There are three possible positions: growing, stable, and declining. Each one presents a different penetration challenge.

1. *Penetrating a growing customer.* A growing customer is sales-driven. If you want to affect the sales function, you must increase its productivity so that it can generate more profits per sale or yield added profits from incremental sales. If you cannot affect sales but you can only reduce costs, the savings you achieve for a customer must be valued for their ability to support more sales. Your entire penetration strategy must focus on improving the customer's profit by increasing sales.

2. *Penetrating a stable customer.* A stable customer is driven from two directions at once. Sales must be increased, but not if it requires increased costs. If projected sales fail to result, the customer's stability can be threatened. Costs must be reduced, but not if it will reduce sales or market share. If sales fall, the customer's stability can be threatened. Your penetration strategy can focus on improving profit through sales increases or cost decreases, but it must avoid the unaffordable risk of increasing costs or decreasing sales in the process.

3. *Penetrating a declining customer.* A declining customer is cost-driven. Increased revenues are unlikely because they are too costly. If you can help lower or eliminate a cost, you can often improve profit on a dollar-for-dollar basis. The dollars that the customer needs to slow the loss of market position will mostly have to come from funds reclaimed from costs. As a result, your penetration strategy must focus on making the customer's cost structure relinquish money for operations.

Positioning Sales Strategies

The purpose of analyzing a customer's business position is to be able to custom-tailor your sales penetration. If a customer is growing or stable, you must present yourself as an improver of profit on sales. If the customer is declining, you must present yourself as a decreaser of costs.

Unless your sales position coincides with the customer's, you will never be able to create a partnership in profit improvement. The customer will not understand where you are coming from in your proposals. You, in turn, lacking a sense of your customer's objectives, will not know where the customer is going. As two unknowns, you will be talking past each other; you will be proposing to yourself.

To ensure that your sales positioning is in gear with how your customer is positioned, your penetration strategy should be preceded by a positioning statement. Here is a model statement:

"In our penetration of the manufacturing functions of the ABC Company's XYZ Division, a stable business, we will position ourselves as the manufacturing vice president's partner in profit improvement primarily by means of the reductions in cost we can deliver through our quality control system. We will also show how enhanced product quality can help improve profit through incremental sales."

Pinpointing Sales Penetration Opportunities

A customer's inability to bring down a cost, and his need to increase profitable sales volume, are major business problems. Accordingly, they can be your sales penetration opportunities. In order to find out, you will have to identify them and then put dollar values on them and on the most cost-effective solutions.

Opportunities to penetrate a key account have a special genesis. A penetration opportunity does not automatically come into being simply because a customer has a problem and you happen to have a solution for it. Discovery is not opportunity. To determine whether a penetration opportunity exists, you must first analyze three specific dollar values.

1. *The dollar value of the customer's problem.* How significant is it? Is it making a significant negative contribution to customer profit? Does it justify a significant expenditure for solution?

2. *The dollar values of the profits from your solution* that will accrue both to you and to your customer. How significant are they? When will they begin to flow? How long before their total amount finally accrues?

3. *The dollar values of the costs of your solution* that will be incurred both by you and by your customer. How significant are they? Are they all up front or can they be paid for progressively out of the solution's improved profits?

Penetration opportunities are entry points. You should regard them as windows. An opportunity window opens for you when the following conditions are met:

1. The dollar value of the profits from your solution exceed the dollar value of the customer's problem.
2. The dollar value of the profits from your solution exceed the dollar value of the costs of your solution.
3. The dollar value of the profits from your solution exceed the dollar value of the profits from competitive solutions.

The first condition ensures that a customer problem is worth solving; that is, it is beneficial to solve. The second condition ensures that a problem is profitable to solve. The third condition ensures that your solution will be the preferred solution. All three conditions place the burden of proof squarely where it belongs—on your ability to create the most profitable solutions to customer problems in the business functions you can affect. This is the supreme standard of performance for Consultative Selling.

Prescribing Systems

A consultant's solutions improve customer profit in proportion to the consultant's skill in prescribing systems. Prescribing is the consultant's highest art. Good consultants are first-rate prescribers. They size up customer needs and specify the most cost-efficient systems to benefit them.

The ability to prescribe the right system the first time is a result of three factors. One is the consultant's experience. The second is expertise. The third factor is skill in solving customer business problems and helping capitalize on opportunities: in other words, helping a customer improve profit.

A system's combined advantage is expressed as a single benefit: profit improvement of the customer's business functions in which the system is installed. This benefit is a partial function of system price. It is also a function of the system's return on investment. The ability of a system to yield a return on investment that exceeds price endows it with premium-price capability.

Prescribing a system and pricing it for high customer return are the two most demanding tasks of Consultative Selling. Together they determine the customer's value and the profit from the system. Because they have such a direct effect on both value and profit, the acts of prescription and pricing are the keystones of the consultant's selling proficiency.

The standard of performance for prescribing and pricing a system is met when the system's premium price is accepted as proof of its added value in meeting customer objectives.

When a consultant prescribes a profit improvement package, it must follow the rule of "necessity and sufficiency." Components must be sufficient, but only those that are necessary to solve the customer's problem should be prescribed. This guideline helps protect consultants against underengineering or overengineering a system. If a system is overengineered, it may have to be overpriced; if it is underengineered, it may contribute to customer dissatisfaction and invite competitive inroads.

To avoid underengineering, you may have to acquire equipment or service components from other manufacturers to round out some systems. At times, it will be possible to market these components under your company's own brand name. This is the preferred way. But even if they cannot be branded, they should nonetheless be incorporated into the system if they are necessary to its objectives.

To be of maximum benefit to your customer and maximum profit to you, a system should have turnover built into it—that is, one or more of its components should be consumable. This allows you to generate an ongoing market for product-related services and consumable supplies, as a means of providing continuing sources of income for your business and continuing sources of knowledge about your customers' businesses.

A basic rule of system prescription can be stated in this way: *To maximize profit, standardize the hardware and customize the services and consumables*. When services and consumables are customized, a system's premium price is justified. When frequent turnover of those consumables is multiplied by premium price, maximum profits can result.

Model Systems Prescriptions

An office communications system. An office communications consultant defines the objective of office systems as improving the profit of customer word processing functions. Business communication is the vital customer process on which the consultant's systems concentrate. To solve problems of rising costs and inefficiencies in communication, the consultant prescribes a total communications system as opposed to the random use of a typewriter here, a dictating machine there, and a word processor and a copying machine somewhere else. The system is composed of input and output processing equipment, together with inspection, maintenance, repair, replacement, resupply, financing, and training services.

A fire protection system. A fire protection consultant defines the objective of fire systems as improving the efficiency and reducing the cost of safeguarding customer's processing functions. The refining of chemicals is the vital customer process on which the consultant's systems concentrate. To solve the problem of rising cost for high-hazard protection, the consultant prescribes a total risk management system as opposed to the random use of a fire extinguisher here, a sprinkler there, and shovels and a bucket of sand somewhere else. The system is composed of fire detection and extinguishing equipment, plus inspection, maintenance, repair, replacement, resupply, financing, and training services.

A materials cleaning system. A materials cleaning consultant defines the objective of cleaning systems as improving the profit of customer electric motor rebuilding processes. Cleaning and repainting electric motors are the vital customer processes on which the consultant's systems concentrate. To solve the problem of rising costs for removing dirt, grease, rust, and paint, the consultant prescribes a total cleaning and finishing system as opposed to the random use of a sandblasting machine here, a blast room there, and steel grit abrasives somewhere else. The system is composed of blasting equipment, consumable abrasives, and related inspection, maintenance, repair, replacement, resupply, financing, and training services.

Responding to Customer Signals

The signal to prescribe a system comes from the customer. It generally takes the form of an objection to a commodity product. There are three major classes of customer objections that can be successfully responded to by prescribing a system:

1. The product is said to be "too expensive" or "no better than the competition."
2. The product requires "frequent servicing" or "sophisticated knowledge" to operate or maintain.

3. The product is subject to "rapid depreciation" or "technological obsolescence."

Systemizing products that are "too expensive" or "no better than competition." When customers perceive a product as too expensive or no better than competition, they are classifying the product as a commodity. Its performance benefits are undifferentiated from those of rival products. It is a utility rather than a branded specialty, offering no proprietary values. Utilities are interchangeable; one supplier's utility is no better or no worse than competitive utilities. Since the only point of difference between utilities is price, customers bargain with suppliers to drive price down as close as possible to cost.

You can usually answer the two objections of expense and competitive parity by embedding your commodity product into a system that contains other products and services. The added values offered by the system as a whole may help justify a premium price. Remember that the system may be able to deliver proprietary benefits that the product alone cannot deliver. It can therefore justify a premium price even though it is built around a commodity product that could not do so alone.

Systemizing products that require frequent servicing or sophisticated knowledge. When a product's normal use requires predictable periodic servicing, consumable replacement parts, or sophisticated operating knowledge, it is a natural candidate for systemizing. This situation is the perfect setting for the classic systems strategy of "the razor and the blades." The razor is the system's "hardware"—the product or equipment. It may be a one-time sale. The blades are the system's "software"—the servicing it requires and the replacement parts and consumables that must be reordered through repeat sales. Over the life cycle of the system, sale of the blades will account for the major contribution to the consultant's income.

The blades also provide a second benefit. They give you continuity with customers. They offer a valid, profitmaking reason to return again and again to monitor the contribution of system performance to a customer's profits. This offers the opportunity to seek out new or further needs that can be supplied, maintain the product's performance so that it operates in the most cost-effective manner, and upgrade the system whenever possible with more sophisticated hardware and accessories.

A razor-and-blades system may include one, two, or all three of the following components:

1. A periodic service agreement to provide recurrent maintenance, repair and replacement parts, and consumables.
2. An education service to teach customer personnel how to operate the system. This service may involve an intensive initial teaching program supplemented by periodic refresher courses in the form of seminars or printed and audiovisual instructional materials, or a school for customers in systems operation and maintenance.
3. An operational service that provides trained personnel employed by the consultant's company to run the system on a cost-plus-fee basis on the customer's premises. The supplier company provides the complete staff and handles its recruitment, compensation, motivation, and benefits.

Systemizing products that are subject to rapid depreciation or technological obsolescence. When a product is subject to rapid depreciation, or if its technology can become rapidly obsolete, it may be difficult to justify a premium price.

If such a product is systemized, it can often be protected from price erosion. The system's added values add to price support. Even though a product may originally be technologically superior, if early obsolescence is in prospect the product should be sold on the more comprehensive benefits of a system. This will provide the supplier with a positioning that may be maintained at length. If, on the other hand, a position is based on the product's temporary technical leadership, premium-price opportunity will be lost as soon as the performance advantages of the product are matched by a competitor.

An extremely important component of a system designed to counter a product's depreciation or technological obsolescence is leasing. If a system can be paid for over time, some of the curse can be taken off depreciation since the system's total price no longer needs to be committed at one time. Because the retained funds can be invested at a return or used in other ways, a lease can endow the consultant's product and the customer's capital funds with added values.

A second benefit of including a lease option in the system for a rapidly depreciating or obsolescent product is that provision can be made within the lease for periodic replacement or upgrading. These services defray the costs of obsolescence by maintaining a system in a state of modernity at all times. When a lease provides this service, it can be promoted as a service-fee method of maintaining the product's original value.

How to Decide Which System to Propose

The return-on-investment approach is the most helpful tool for determining which of two or more systems to propose to a customer as well as how to price. A simple example will illustrate this point.

- *System A* is forecast to improve customer sales by $200,000 and yield a profit on sales of 10 percent, or $20,000. The investment required from the customer is $100,000.
- *System B* is forecast to improve customer sales by $300,000 and yield a profit on sales of 10 percent, or $30,000. The same $100,000 of customer investment will be required.

These two systems appear equally worthwhile in terms of their 10 percent profit yield on sales. But in terms of the return each system can achieve on the amount of customer capital it employs, System B is superior. With System B, $100,000 of capital can produce a $30,000 profit—a 30 percent return. System A also requires $100,000 of capital but can produce only $20,000 in profit, for a 20 percent return.

The difference between the two is the relationship of the improved sales volume to the capital employed. System A allows its capital to appreciate at the rate of 200 percent. With System B, however, the appreciation is 300 percent: it turns inventories into cash faster.

There is a shorthand formula you can use to determine return on investment:

$$\frac{\text{Profit}}{\text{Sales}} \times \frac{\text{sales}}{\text{capital employed}} = \text{\% return on investment (ROI)}$$

In the case of System A:

$$\frac{20{,}000}{200{,}000} \times \frac{200{,}000}{100{,}000} = 20\% \text{ ROI}$$

In the case of System B:

$$\frac{30{,}000}{300{,}000} \times \frac{300{,}000}{100{,}000} = 30\% \text{ ROI}$$

In this simplified approach, the first fraction calculates the percentage of profit on sales; the second fraction calculates the turnover rate. When the two are multiplied, the result is return on investment.

Any improvement in the circulation of funds invested in a system's total assets, working assets, or any component part of an individual asset will have a multiplying effect on profits.

The Customer Advantage

A system's marketability lies in its "customer advantage," the value added by improving customer profit. This customer advantage becomes the system advantage in the minds of customers, who evaluate systems both individually and competitively. A system does more than offer a customer advantage; the system comes to "own" the advantage as its single most crucial selling point. This is *preemption,* a system's ability to seize an advantage uniquely to itself.

The preempted advantage of a system acts as its market selecting mechanism. It selects customers in two ways. First, it seeks out and qualifies the segment of a market that has the greatest need for the system's advantage. Second, it comes to represent the system by acting as a shorthand way of describing its incremental contribution. The customer advantage determines the market and documents the system's capabilities.

A system's customer advantage must conform to three requirements:

1. It must confer a superior added value over competitive systems, as well as over the option of doing nothing, in at least one important respect.
2. It must be at least equal to competitive systems in all other respects.
3. It must not be inferior to competitive systems in any important respect.

A preemptive advantage can be an attribute of the system. Or it can come from the way it is implemented, maintained, migrated, or marketed. The question of how much quality to build into a system therefore merits a minimal answer. Enough quality to deliver the customer advantage is enough quality. A maximum quality system as determined by the aggregate quality of its components may not be perceived as offering the maximum customer advantage. Minimal systems from the consultant's perspective are often preemptive systems from the customer's perspective.

The concept of preemption of customer advantage is not just an argument against overengineering, overpackaging, or overcosting, although it speaks powerfully against all three. It is essentially an argument in favor of prescribing systems from a customer orientation. And it provides the direction for establishing a system's branding: the capture of customer preference because the *customer's profit is being improved best,* not because the *consultant's system is constructed best.*

Defending Against Desystemizing

A consultant's prescription for improved customer profit is always threatened by desystemizing. You should not fear the process. It plays the vital role of confirming the value of your prescriptive expertise and your ability to apply it to a customer's problems.

The essential consultative value is the ability to *apply*. This is what a prescription really is—an application of the consultant's expertise to a customer's business.

To this extent, you are an applications consultant. All the professional expertise in the world is valueless unless you can apply it to a customer's business. By protecting a system against customer attempts to desystemize it, you learn the extent of your prescriptive and applications skills.

Challenges to desystemize a system are actually a customer's attempt to test the worth of your applications expertise, which is the trump card that justifies premium price. Desystemizing is a price reduction strategy. Since premium price lies at the heart of Consultative Selling strategy, the system must be protected if premium price is to be maintained.

A system is only as good as its consultant's applications ability. Unless the consultant's expertise can be *branded*—that is, accepted as providing a value that exceeds its price and that cannot be obtained elsewhere—a system cannot be protected from customer attempts to desystemize it.

There are two basic desystemizing strategies:

1. Attempts to acquire only certain components of a system.
2. Attempts to acquire only the consultant's prescriptive expertise and information base.

When a customer threatens to desystemize your system, you have recourse to two strategies. One is the "yes" defense, which is effective against the only-certain-components attack. The other is the "no" defense, which is effective against the only-the-prescription-and-information-components attack.

The "Yes" Defense

A customer who does not want to pay premium price for a system but who still sees value in some of its components will try to cherry-pick. This is often like the Chinese-restaurant approach of selecting one from Column A and one from Column B. When a system is attacked in piecemeal fashion, the best protective strategy is to say yes. There are three reasons:

1. *You make a sale.* A partial sale is usually better than no sale at all. Penetration is established. At least some income is earned to pay off a portion of the sales cost.

2. *You have a foot in the door.* Even a partial sale gets you involved with a customer. This gives you an opportunity to apply upgrading sales strategies that can gradually result in your selling an entire system with additional components. This is the way many partial systems become full systems. In most businesses, customers tend to stick with their original system suppliers. Up to 90 percent of many systems sales come from add-on purchases by existing customers.

3. *You can gain information.* Every customer problem that is solved yields new information about the customer and the customer's markets. A new cost center may be found. A new way of reducing it may be discovered. A new sales opportunity may be identified. A new way of seizing it may be tried. Each time, something new will be learned to suggest the next proposal.

From these three reasons for saying yes to a customer, it is apparent that agreement to sell part of a system must be tempered by one consideration: the brandable components of a system must never be compromised. No matter what components are agreed on, the consultant's prescriptive expertise in profit improvement and the information base on which it depends must always be included in the sale.

In Figure 6-1, a consultant's recommended responses to customer requests are tabulated. They relate to the materials cleaning system proposed back in Figure 3-2. Even though the components of the system are specific to materials cleaning, the responses are typical for all systems.

Figure 6-1. Responses to desystemizing.

System Components	*Recommended Seller's Responses to Customer Desystemizing*
Swing table, blast-cleaning machine, and worktable	Yes
Operating supplies, including steel grit abrasives, and replacement parts	Yes
Environmental control: fabric filter dust collector to prevent in-plant and outside air pollution	Yes
Operating personnel training program on cost-effective operation and maintenance	Yes
Periodic inspection and maintenance-monitoring service	Yes
Profit improvement planning service to reduce cost and improve profit from materials cleaning process	No
Customer information service on applying new developments in the technology of blast cleaning, equipment, components, and supplies	No

The "No" Defense

The most dangerous attack against a system is the attempt to select out its APDAB components: the consultant's *applications expertise and database*. This probe must be resisted at all costs. The consultant's expertise and data resources are your rock-bottom leverage against desystemization. If they can be obtained separately, there may be no incentive left for the customer to acquire the total system. But the key reason for protecting expertise and information is that their premium values support the umbrella of premium price over the entire consultative system. Without them, a system will degenerate into a commodity.

The best defense against this type of desystemizing is to identify the consultant's expertise and information with the system as a whole. "After all," you may reason with a customer, "my prescriptive expertise is based on managing systems composed of my company's equipment and services. I know these components. I have confidence in them. I can predict their contribution to improved profit. To ask me to apply my expertise to a system of foreign components deprives me of my quality control. It may defeat my ability and nullify my experience. It will certainly devalue my information base, which, as you know, has been painstakingly built up from experience with my own equipment and services in solving a wide range of problems. It may not be valid for other suppliers' systems. For these reasons, I must say *no*."

No consultant likes to say no to a customer. Yet the desystemizing strategy of selecting only the consultant's expertise and information strikes so directly at the systems concept that there is no choice. It must be rejected. The only way to avoid answering with a "no" response is to see that it is not provoked in the first place. This is your principal educational task.

You can always be certain of two facts about a system. For one, no matter how novel the hardware components may be initially, they will eventually become commodities. For this reason, you cannot allow customers to regard hardware as the core of your systems. Second, the only component that can be branded against commodity status is the "software" represented by your own prescriptive and applications expertise. Every consultant must educate customers to accept this basic truth from the very beginning. This is not easily reconciled when hardware is exclusive, innovative, technologically sophisticated, and personally exciting to the consultant and even to customers. Nonetheless, it must be done. It is your only strategy for avoiding the recurrent need to say no and to redirect customer attention to saying yes to profit improvement.

Consultative Partnering Strategies

7

How to Set Partnerable Objectives

Every business has natural partners. Who are yours? They are other businesses whose growth is dependent on you. Selecting your growth partners is the single most important act of Consultative Selling.

If you know who your natural partners are and what they need from you in order to grow, you can dedicate your Profit Improvement Proposals to them from the outset. Your business positioning can be a natural response to theirs. Your system capabilities can be exactly receptive to their needs. Your database can contain knowledge of their growth problems and opportunities. Your entire business can be the reciprocal of the businesses of your partners.

You have two types of natural growth partners. One is composed of businesses that are currently growing because of you. The other is composed of businesses that you could grow but are not currently growing.

Choosing Current Customers to Partner With

There are four questions to answer about your current customers in order to determine which of them you should partner with:

Who are you growing right now? Some of your growth partners will be customers you are already growing. You may not be aware of your contribution to their growth. You may think you are merely selling to them. But they are actually partners without portfolio. In order to determine whether any one of them should be selected as your partner, you will have to answer three more questions.

How much are they growing you? You may be unable to know the full extent to which you are bringing growth to a current customer. But you can much more easily calculate the profits by which you are growing as a result of the customer's business with you. There are four standards by which you should measure profits: their absolute value, their comparative value ranked against your customer list as a whole, their rate of growth, and the trend of their growth rate over the past three years.

How much more can you grow them? Growth takes place in the future. Consequently, you must add a fifth standard to your calculations: what is the most likely projected rate of improved profits you can plan for in the growth of their business over the next three years? If the projected rate of growth is becoming static or in decline, you may not have a true growth partner. Instead, you may have a mature customer to whom you continue to vend products at competitive prices, whom you should sell to and profit from but not partner.

How much more can they grow you? Because growth partnerships must be reciprocal, you must evaluate the most likely projected rate of your own profit growth over the next three years to see whether it is increasing, becoming static, or entering decline. If the projected incremental rates of growth are increasing for both your customer's and your own business, you have the ideal basis for growth partnering.

Choosing Prospective Partners

There are three questions to answer about prospective partners in order to determine which of them you should partner with:

Who else can you grow? Growable businesses that you are not currently growing are your source of consultative expansion. In order to qualify as a growable customer, a business must meet two criteria. Its business function problems must be susceptible to significant cost reduction by the application of your expertise. In addition, your expertise must be able to increase the customer's own profitable sales opportunities.

How much will they grow you? A business that is growable by you must also be able to grow you in return if it is to be partnerable. Its contribution to your profit volume and its projected three-year rate of growth must meet or exceed your company's minimum growth requirements. These will typically be 20 percent or more per year.

How can you grow them? For each growable customer that you determine is potentially partnerable, you must plan a growth strategy.

The strategy will set forth the precise means by which you will add new profits to the customer's business. You will need to specify how much profit will accrue from reducing business function costs, how soon its flow will begin, and how long it will continue. You will also have to specify the amount and flow of profit from new sales opportunities that you can make available and the markets they can be expected to come from.

The businesses you are growing and businesses you are able to grow are the keys to your growth. The very fact of their growth or growability identifies them as consumers of cash. They are heavy users of money to finance their growth. If you can become an improver of their profits, you can become important to them as a money source.

Not only do they need cash, they need cash fast. They must channel it back into the two major cash-hungry functions of their business that control, or would otherwise constrain, their continued growth: manufacturing and sales. If you become an improver of their profits, you can become important to them as a source of fast cash flow.

Fine-Tuning Criteria

Growability must be your key partnering objective. Only by growing can your partner ensure a fast turnover of your sales and their prolonged continuance. This requires a high turnover in the sales your customer makes to his own customers. If they become stable, turnover will stagnate. For this reason, stable customers—especially those with large shares of market that cannot be grown—are to be avoided. They make good customers but they are poor partners.

If you have a choice among growable customers—customers who meet your primary objective—what fine-tuning criteria should you apply to select among them? You should look for three attributes:

1. *Nascent opportunity*. You should seek the maximum opportunity to grow and be grown. Change is the mother of opportunity. A growable customer that is undergoing reorganization or restructuring to provide for further expansion offers enhanced partnership prospects. Change at the top tier is an added enhancement. Whenever major change is taking place, you have the chance to create a new role for yourself, meet new or newly perceived needs in new ways, and form relationships with new managers who can benefit significantly from your expertise.

2. *Positive attitude*. You should prefer to partner with customers who prefer to partner. Their receptivity to your overtures will be

greater. So will their awareness of and concern for growth. At the minimum, you should expect them to be willing to share data with you and to create a correlate profit improvement team to work with yours.

3. *High repute*. You should understand that the most sophisticated customers make the best partners. They will have the highest standards of performance. That will push you. They will have the most intelligent managers in their industry. That will pull you. Your contribution to them will most likely be maximized; they will take what you give them and run with it. Your odds for a successful track record will increase, as will your ability to draw on them for references that will attract other sophisticated customers to you.

Partnering requires more than just your own choice. Your customers must also choose. Why should they partner with you?

First, you must be an important source of growth profits. Your contribution of new assets must be significant. You must be able to deliver them in timely fashion, recognizing the time value of money. You must also be dependable. Your importance will be in direct proportion to your reliability.

Second, you must be one of the best investments in profit growth. When a growth partner does business with you, the price is an investment rather than a cost. The distinction between the two is vital: only an investment yields a return. The customer invests not in your products or services or systems, not even in your solutions. Investment is justified only by the new profits that you can install in the customer's business. The return from investment with you must be among the highest yields the customer can earn.

The Ground Rules of Partnering

Maintaining partners imposes three requirements:

1. *You must participate*. You must be actively involved with your customers, working closely with them to learn how to help solve their business problems. This means more than just proposing and selling. It means finding out when and where they want you to get involved with their problems and then getting into them at that point. It means investing up-front time to study their situations, laying down your fact base before proceeding into the selling cycle, and building your acceptance within their organizations on a step-by-step basis.

2. *You must commit*. You must plan a long-term growth relationship with each key account, viewing it as an essential part of your business. Your own people and your customer's people must both

know your commitment. It should be in your standards of performance and your allocations of time to key customers.

3. *You must measure*. You must agree with your customer decisionmakers on the criteria you will use together to take periodic readings on your progress in improving customer profits. There can be no appreciation of accomplishment without knowledge in advance about how it will be determined. The criteria of performance and profit that will be used must be laid down at the start. So must the measurement tools that will be used to read the criteria. Just as good fences make good neighbors, good measuring standards make good partners.

Common Denominators of Partnering

All partnering is based on a few common denominators:

- Partners have a *common objective*. Each partner wants to improve profit.
- Partners have *common strategies* for achieving their objective. Their methods are based on mutual need-seeking and mutual need fulfillment. In both cases, needs are arrived at through negotiation.
- Partners are at *common risk*. Each partner has something of value to gain or lose.
- Partners have a *common defense* against all others who are not included in the partnership. Each party deals as an equal. Outsiders range from being less equal to being perceived as competitors.

Cooperative negotiation strategies enable partners to treat each other as equals. This is the principal rule of partnerships. There are ten additional rules that can help in partnering:

1. Add value to each other. Teach each other new ways to improve personal achievement and professional productivity so that both partners profit by the relationship.
2. Be supportive of each other, not competitive. Form a staunch team.
3. Avoid surprises. Plan work together and work according to plan.
4. Be open and aboveboard. Always level with each other.

5. Enter into each other's frame of reference. Learn each other's perceptions in order to see things from the other's point of view. Learn each other's assumptions to understand the other's expectations of the partnership.
6. Be reliable. Partners must be there for each other when they are needed.
7. Anticipate opportunities and capitalize on them. Forecast problems and steer the partnership around them. Keep the partnership out of trouble. If trouble is unavoidable, give the partnership a head start in solving it.
8. Do homework. Know what's happening. Know what may happen.
9. Treat each other as people, not just as functionaries. Be willing to provide the personal "little extras" that make a partnership a humane as well as a mighty force.
10. Enjoy the relationship and make it enjoyable. Both partners should prefer to work within the partnership rather than within any other relationship because it is one of the most rewarding associations either of them has ever had.

In Consultative Selling, partners share improved profit. This is the partnership's prime benefit. The second major benefit that partners can confer on each other is learning together just how their profits can be improved. A partnership should be a breeding ground for generating new knowledge of profitmaking and putting it to work with shared faith and apprehension. The act of learning together is one of the strongest bonding agents in a partnership. It is the growth element in the relationship because it ensures that *both* partners will grow.

The third attribute of a successful partnership is mutual support. Each partner takes on the parts of the relationship's labor that best fit individual capabilities. The complementary nature of the relationship enhances each of them. Conversely, each partner is diminished by the absence of the other.

Understanding a Partner's Motivations

The customer decisionmakers who must be partnered are multimotivated. They rarely act on the basis of one motive alone. Status, money, autonomy, and self-realization propel them. Of all their drives, three are likely to be major: power, achievement, and affiliation.

The power motive. Managers like to direct, influence, and control others. They like power. Power is measured by three standards: control over important resources; the ability to impose will on others; and the extent to which the flow of events can be influenced. Power can give its holder the right to act or to prevent others from acting. Power *over* people, or power *with* them, is called leadership.

The consultant must learn to cope with the power structure in customer organizations. Power can be recognized by its two faces. One is *personalized;* the other is *socialized*. Personalized power is based on a dominance-submission relationship, a win-lose type of interaction. It is self-aggrandizing at the expense of others. Socialized power, on the other hand, is used for the benefit of others. It helps make people feel confident and competent so that they can achieve common objectives. It is energizing, sustaining, and supportive.

The achievement motive. Managers are typically high achievers. They are task-oriented: they initiate action rather than reacting. It is not money, power, or a need for the respect of their associates that primarily drives them. It is the urge to achieve for its own sake. Consultants who are also high achievers should find it mutually rewarding to negotiate with fast-track customer managers.

The affiliation motive. Both the power motive and the affiliation motive are geared to people. While power involves dominance, affiliation involves relating to other people in ways that maintain good interpersonal relations. The affiliation motive is people-oriented. Most effective managers rate high on affiliation, expressing their drive to relate to others with whom they identify. This is also true of the best consultants.

Your Objectives with Customers

What must your objectives be with customers? First, you must help them extend their power by improving performance, increasing their visibility as cost-effective managers, and supporting their claim to promotion. Second, you must help them achieve: achieve more, achieve more importantly, and achieve more consistently. Third, you must help them become identified as high achievers so that other high achievers will affiliate with them.

Each of these objectives is in keeping with objectives of your own as a business grower, an improver of profits as well as an improver of the customer's managers who have profit responsibility.

8

How to Agree on Partnerable Strategies

A consultant's job can be defined in three ways: bring back sales, bring back customer information that can lead to sales, and leave behind alliances with top tier decisionmakers.

Sometimes a sale will build an alliance. More often, alliances help build sales.

There are four levels on which alliances must be structured in a key customer account. Three of them are in the upper management tier. The fourth is the purchasing level, where the traditional adversary relationship must be converted into a more partnerable affiliation.

The objectives of all key account alliances are similar, regardless of the level at which they are to be achieved. Their overriding goal is to ensure customer continuity. Unless key account relationships are continuous, there will be no way to maximize the profit opportunity that a major customer represents. Unless you can keep your key customers, everything else is academic.

Alliance-Building Strategies

Three strategies will help you build lasting alliances: collaborate, educate, and negotiate.

Collaborate. In key account situations, it takes two to make every sale. An unpartnered consultant cannot sell within a customer's company. There will be no one to sell *to*. There will be no one to sell *with*. There will be no one to *help sell*. For consultant and collaborator, there must be the same dedication, the same commitment, and the same conviction that a sale will add genuine values to both parties. When a sale is finally made, it should be impossible to tell who made it. This is the test of a true collaboration: The sale is the thing, not the seller.

Educate. You and your key customers must do more than buy and sell if your relationships are to be continuous. Along with making new dollars, you should both be making new information available to the people on each side who will be collaborating on proposing sales. Not only must you both *earn* as a result of your relationships, you must both *learn* as well. Professional growth and personal growth should attend profit growth.

Negotiate. The main subject area of the mutual education between collaborators is how to improve profits. This requires continuing back-and-forth dialog. The flow of input must be unimpeded. The ideal environment will be rich in options—but sparse in negative thinking, put-downs, editorializing, or defensiveness against anything that is "not invented here." Free-swinging relationships where there is a high degree of give and take allow you and your customers to avoid losing out on important opportunities. They also allow you to cash in fully on solving the problems that come off the top of the customer's head.

Alliances with Top Managers

By selling as a consultant, you obtain access up and down the entire vertical chain of a customer's organization, perhaps including the chief operating officer, who is usually the president. If you sell to a division or subsidiary of a large customer company, your top ally may be its president. Selling to several divisions or to the corporate management itself will require you to partner at the top company level as well as at top divisional levels.

Customer presidents will join in alliances with key account representatives if, but only if, their self-interest is engaged. At their level, there are three principal interests:

1. *Financial improvement.* Chief operating officers are mainly preoccupied with bottom-line profits. They view their businesses as money machines. For most of their daily routine, they are on the lookout for as many ways as possible to convert investments—their allocation of resources—into superior return. If you can position yourself with them in this context, they can include your system among their investment options.

Presidents focus on returns. Their accountability to various constituencies demands it. Employees, shareholders, directors, and securities analysts all lean on them to produce increased profits. In selling to presidents in a consultative manner, you can help relieve some of this pressure. In your consultative role, you represent an added chance for them to earn new profits.

2. *People improvement.* Although presidents are fixated on returns, they never lose sight of where returns come from. Profits are made by people; they are a president's prime capital resource. If you can help improve the knowledge, competence, and productivity of strategically placed customer people, you can ally yourself as a partner in a major presidential mission.

What can customer people learn from you? You can improve their ability to reduce the costs of their operations so that they will become less of a drain on internal funds, or require a lower investment in their operations. You can also improve their ability to enhance sales revenues. If their abilities are upgraded in these vital areas, their profit contributions can be increased and their productivity stepped up by the amount they add to revenues for each dollar of investment in them.

3. *Operational improvement.* All customer operations are cost centers. By their nature, only a few can ever become profit centers. If you can bring down a cost center's asset base by streamlining its operations, consolidating functions, eliminating steps in its processes, or reducing its need for labor, energy, or materials, you can create a common interest with customer presidents.

Presidents often ask themselves—and they are often asked by others—"How competitive are we?" By this, they mean many things: How good are our people, our products, our promotion? They also run an ongoing audit of their operations to determine how competitive they are. They call it productivity. It provides a useful index of just how effectively their operations are converting a dollar of investment into a dollar of sales.

When you help presidents improve their functions' productivity, you are assisting them in making their own businesses more competitive; that is, you are joining with them to help maintain their profitability, add to it, or regain it. These are always among the most paramount issues confronting decisions at the top tier.

Vendor sales representatives remain largely unaware of potential interfaces with customer presidents. Even if they have the awareness, they lack the ability to implement it so they can form alliances. They are often obsessed with a desire to "get upstairs." But it is the wrong obsession. The true objective is to be able to form a continuing alliance upstairs so that you can go back again and again—indeed, so that your presence will be regarded as an ongoing added value by customer people at the top.

Because vendors are unable to relate to customer presidents—what would they talk about, their own product?—many of them regard a presidential alliance as a preposterous assumption. In reality, it has a recognizable basis in fact. People at a customer's top tier are immersed every day in selling situations with their president. Everyone from top and middle management levels approaches the president with something to sell: a new business venture or new product idea, an expansion of staff or facilities, or a new market penetration. Top tier managers approach presidents and their committees in a consultative mode: they request appropriations on the basis of their ability to contribute a superior return.

This is the only way to approach the top, because it is the only way the top approaches investing its funds. When you sell as a consultant, you must replicate the approach that is comfortable to top decision-makers. Vendors, however, ask management to buy price performance. Not only is top management unskilled in making this type of commitment, it is also uncomfortable at being asked to play a purchasing role. Appropriately enough, it sends vendors back downstairs.

Alliances with Financial Managers

Customer financial managers, either controllers or financial vice presidents, share their presidents' criteria for evaluating the desirability of major purchases. They, too, are motivated by return on investment. Forming alliances at their level will require, for the most part, a similar strategy.

Financial managers regard themselves as keepers of the corporate checkbook. In that capacity, they are just as concerned as their top managers about preserving capital. Even more than presidents, though, they focus on what goes out. They tend to be highly cost-conscious, auditing with exactitude the amounts of investment required to achieve a return as well as the size, timing, and certainty of the return itself. As the "point men" for the corporate struggle for funds, they more than anyone else are aware of the horns of the dilemma posed by an investment situation: What if I make the investment? Will a better one come along tomorrow after I am out of funds? What if I don't make the investment? Suppose a better one does not come along?

It is understandable that financial managers are cautious. If they are approached with a vendor's characteristic persuasiveness, their inherent defenses will be heightened. They find a safe haven in numbers—the financial facts of a proposition to buy. Numbers are their words. They speak of "reading" them, letting the numbers "tell" them things, and getting their "message." In order to partner with them, you must talk to them in their own language.

Financial managers are called money managers for good reason. Money is their unit of communication. For them, it talks. It converses with them in terms of its rate of return, its discounted cash flow, and its present value. Financial managers are always in the market for money. They want to invest it, to put it to work for their businesses so that it will earn more money, which in turn will give them more money to invest, and so on. They are the customer's investment managers. To form alliances with them, you will have to provide them with new investment opportunities in the form of profit proposals.

Controllers and directors of customer financial functions never lack for places to put money to work in their businesses. What they do lack, however, is the funds themselves. If you are going to have relevance for them as an ally, it will hardly ever be due to your products or services, unless they can be used in the operations of the financial function itself. Your relevance will depend on the new investment dollars you can produce and how quickly and dependably they can be obtained.

Alliances with Functional Managers

Customer business function managers are immersed in the problems of supervising and administering their operations. They live in a world of people problems, productivity problems, manufacturing problems, quality control problems, inventory control problems, sales problems; whatever their function happens to be, it will have several of these problems as a normal consequence of its day-to-day activities. Business function managers always seek relief from their problems. They want their attendant costs removed. They want their opportunities expanded for greater sales revenues and productivity.

As a result, they want to be knowledgeable in three areas:

1. *How to improve their operations*. What options exist for improvement, how they work to deliver improvement, and what mix of options will provide the optimal results.
2. *When to improve their operations*. What timing is optimal for the introduction of improvements, how they can best be se-

quenced, and when the payoff on an improvement can be expected.

3. *Where to improve their operations*. What parts of their processes are the best starting points, how they can be improved most cost-effectively, and where an improvement can next be migrated so that its impact can be multiplied.

Remembering these principal concerns, it is easy to understand why approaching functional managers by trying to sell them your product or service is unlikely to make a sale. Nowhere in their areas of concern is a concern for your products. They care only for how products can affect their operations and when and where to implement them. Their functions are the context for judging what fits and what doesn't, what works and what won't, what is a good buy and what isn't.

The vendor sales approach that says "I want to sell you something" is meaningless when it is directed to a business function manager. It is, literally, out of context; that is, it has no perceived relation to the business function. To say "I would like to work with you" is equally meaningless. The only approach that makes sense is the consultative approach: "I can help improve your operation, both in performance and in profit." This addresses the business function manager's concept of a problem. It also addresses the function manager in your consultative role as profit-improver.

Alliances with Purchasing Managers

The traditional interests of purchasing managers cannot be addressed in consultative alliances. Competitive price performance considerations are not the consultant's stock in trade. Instead, a new set of standards must be introduced into the purchasing relationship, to upgrade its areas of concern to parallel those held by business function managers. Value considerations must replace price. The financial aspects of performance must be substituted for physical, chemical, mechanical, hydraulic, or electronic performance results as buying criteria. Benefits must be recast in dollar terms from the traditional measurements of pounds, gallons, bytes, or man-days.

Alliances with purchasing management have two objectives. The first is to create a consultative partnership that will enable you and your customer purchasers to develop profit improvement proposals in collaboration with each other. Then, together you can take them upstairs for joint presentations at the top tier.

The second objective of a purchasing alliance is to develop an implementation exchange. As outsiders, you can help purchasers by providing access to information and access to higher-level management inside their organization, and by educating them in the profit improvement approach to evaluating proposals. Because purchasers are corporate insiders, they can help you with internal data on customer needs, decisionmaking practices, and the politics of functional management relations. In these ways, the basis for partnership exists. It will not be easy to cultivate. But it cannot be ignored. To go over or around the purchasers with whom you have a vendor relationship will leave a score to be settled later on and an enemy where there might have been an ally.

Partnering with Negotiation

Negotiation is the consultant's main penetration strategy. It is the act of mutual bargaining over optional ways of achieving a common objective. When the objective is reached, both negotiators win. The customer wins the profit improvement benefits from the consultant's system. The consultant wins the profit improvement benefits from selling or leasing it.

Negotiation is a reciprocal process. Both parties must develop the customer's needs. Then both parties must discuss the best way the customer's needs can be fulfilled while at the same time making sure that the consultant's needs are also fulfilled. Because consultant and customer develop the customer's needs together, the climate of a negotiated sale is we-oriented from the beginning. It says to the customer that *we* are both concerned with serving *your needs*.

When the customer's needs are revealed to both the customer and the consultant and when it can be shown that those needs are served best by the consultant's system, both of them know that their individual self-interests will be met.

To penetrate a customer organization by negotiation, you must understand three aspects of the negotiation process:

1. Negotiation requires a win-win orientation. Both you and the customer must win a benefit.
2. Negotiation requires that both consultant and customer perceive each other as equals. Each must hold equal respect for the other as an essential contributor to the fulfillment of their common objective.

3. Negotiation requires that both consultant and customer lay their needs on the table and that they then proceed to satisfy the customer's needs in the way that is best for both of them.

You must manage the give and take of the negotiation process by which the customer's needs are learned. It is your job to take charge of the process. The best way you can conduct a consultative sale is to practice the art of negotiative questioning with customers. There are six basic types of negotiating questions:

1. *Why* questions that ask the customer: "Why do you manage your operation the way you do?"
2. *What if* questions that ask the customer: "What if certain things were done in a different way?"
3. *How* questions that ask the customer: "How do you feel about current results? How might your operations be conducted in a more cost-effective manner?"
4. *Who* questions that ask the customer: "Who could benefit most from change? Who might be hurt or inconvenienced? Whose ox would be gored?"
5. *When* questions that ask the customer: "When will a proposal be best timed so that it will have the greatest chance for acceptance? When must the onset of profit flow begin?"
6. *Where* questions that ask the customer: "Where can I gain access to the internal information I require? Where can I validate the external information I have acquired?"

Consultant-Customer Motivation Sets

In the course of having their needs developed through negotiation, customers will have their first experience in being a partner. From it, they will derive their first impressions of your consultative skills. This impression forms the basis for respect. From the same experience, customers also derive their first impressions of your knowledge of their business and how to improve their profits. This impression forms the basis for confidence. To initiate customers into partnership, you must become aware of customer needs and how they differ from your own.

The Consultant's Need Set

There are three aspects of consultant needs. Each represents a certain type of income: *money income; psychic income,* representing such rewards as power, prestige, and promotion; and *self-actualization income,* including self-fulfillment, competence, and the realization of talent potential.

These needs are present in every consultant's motivation set. Yet they vary widely from one consultant to another. To negotiate effectively, your need set must be proportioned something like Figure 8-1. The power aspect of your income must necessarily be small. Although you may enjoy great prestige, you will always be required to work through your customer to accomplish your purposes. You can help a customer achieve power and promotion and thereby share vicariously in these income sources. But you will often work unheralded, usually anonymously.

Consultants, on the other hand, must also have an unusually large

Figure 8-1. Consultant motivation set.

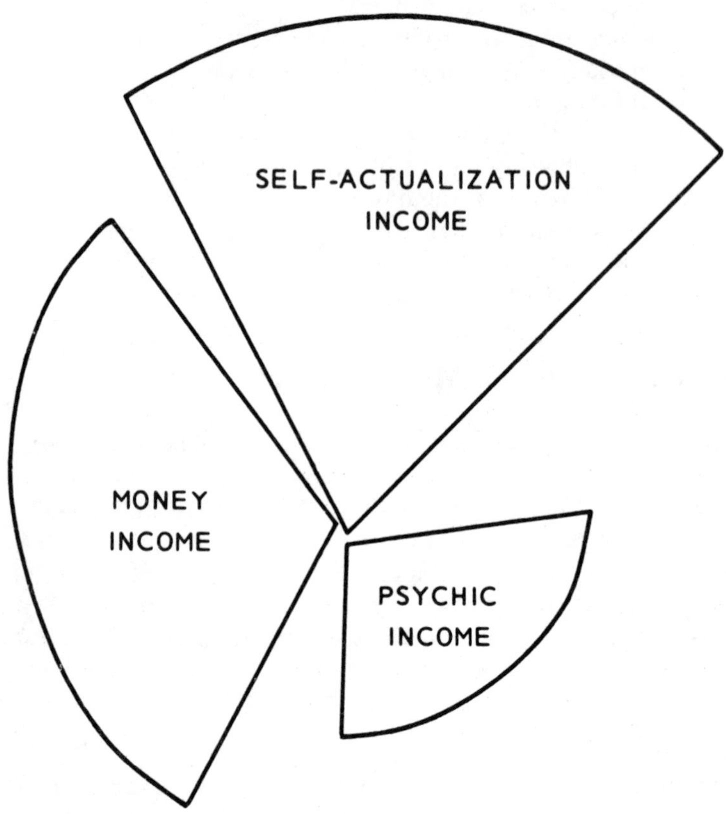

amount of self-actualization in their need set. This aspect is the key to success. You must have, and be driven by, a need to realize your own fullest growth and development. You must want to utilize all of yourself in your customer's behalf, engaging your full complement of skills and expressing your widest range of knowledge. You must need to translate these qualities into unique profit projects that could have come from you alone and that bear the unmistakable imprint of your personal style.

The Customer's Need Set

In Figure 8-2, three aspects of customer needs are illustrated in typical proportion. They contrast with the proportions shown in Figure 8-1 for the consultant's need set. The major difference lies in the relative significance of self-actualization income and psychic income. For the consultant, self-actualization must always take precedence over the psychic rewards of power, prestige, and promotion. For the customer, however, you should assume that power and promotion—which represent realizable objectives for a customer—supersede self-fulfillment. By remembering the primacy of power and promotion when you negotiate, you will be able to keep your customer's perspective in mind. You will also be able to visualize your role fairly accu-

Figure 8-2. Customer motivation set.

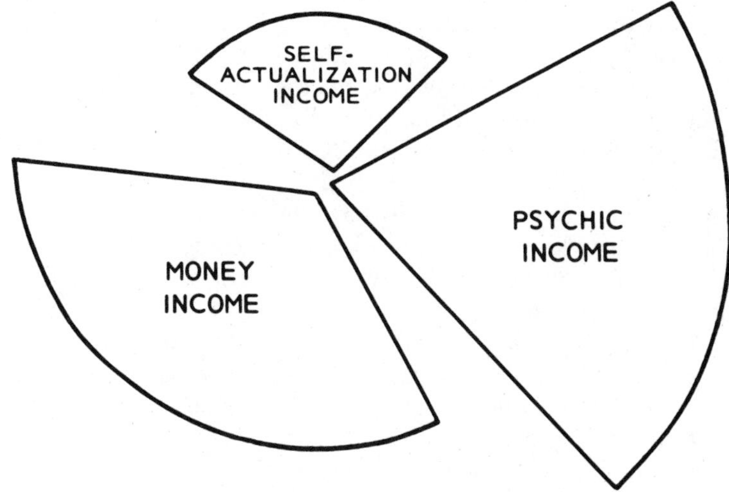

rately in the way the customer will see it: to help the customer obtain increased power income and maximize money income as well.

You must achieve harmony in your relationships by integrating your needs with those of your customer. The initiative must be yours. It is your task to perceive yourself, first of all, in the power-accelerator role that your customer perceives for you. Second, you must devote your own self-actualization motives to your customer's best interests. And third, you must adopt a posture of empathy with your customer so that both need sets can operate as one.

How to Negotiate with Power Sources

The different needs of consultant and customer determine the negotiation process that bonds their partnership.

The ability to make decisions is solely within the customer's power. The consultant has no comparable power. Your only leverage against a customer's power is the ability to improve customer profit. With this ability, you can influence customer decisions. This means two things. You must know everything that is knowable about how a profit-improving system can be designed to meet customer needs. You must also know everything that is knowable about the customer's power structure.

Power is the ability to make, prevent, or influence a decision. Very few decisionmakers have that much power. Instead, power is typically limited and fragmented. You must find out who has what type of power. Only then can a Consultative Selling strategy be planned. It will be helpful for you to seek out three power sources:

1. *The power to say yes.* A yes-sayer is your prime partner. If you can identify a yes-sayer's needs and influence them directly on a one-to-one basis, the maximum opportunity will exist for selling.

2. *The power to say no.* A no-sayer is your prime potential adversary. A no-sayer does not generally have the power to say yes, but may have the power to kill a proposal before it can come to the attention of a yes-sayer. To sell consultatively, you will have to neutralize no-sayers or convert them into allies.

3. *The power to influence the yes-sayers and the no-sayers.* An influencer has only implicit power. But that power can often swing the balance of decisionmaking in your favor. Influencers can be especially important in helping override a no-sayer's objections. Your task is to mobilize an influencer's influence in a way that helps you sell.

How to Deal with Yes-Sayers

Yes-sayers have official power, the power of position. It is usually symbolized by a title that expresses power to compel compliance.

Appeals to a yes-sayer should be based on the projected improvements in profit that your system can contribute to the yes-sayer's operations. There are two supplementary appeals to which yes-sayers are usually responsive. The first is an appeal to maintain the organization's image of efficiency, modernity, and quality in the minds of its customers, competitors, employees, investors, and other constituents. The second is an appeal to the yes-sayer's personal need to manage a significant process improvement, preside over a respected and well-reputed operation, and take prudent risks.

Here is a checklist of appeals to yes-sayers:

1. Profit improvement and increased cost-effectiveness.
2. Improved organizational image for operating efficiency, modern methods, leading-edge technology, and quality.
3. Compatibility of a system's benefits with personal values such as being on top of things, managing in a progressive fashion, and being a wise evaluator of innovation.

How to Deal with No-Sayers

No-sayers often have official power; they may be second in command and report to a yes-sayer. Or they may have a political power base unheralded by a high title. Sometimes they are deliberately encouraged by a yes-sayer to perform a control function by acting as devil's advocates.

No-sayers perceive their roles as saying no. When they are unable to find any reason to say no, they use their favorite word anyway even in giving tacit agreement: "I can find *no* reason not to go ahead." You must communicate with no-sayers in their own terms. They must be deprived of any reason to say no and still be allowed to fully exercise their negative approach.

This means that you will have to demonstrate point by point why there is no reason that your system should not be employed. This may require infinitely detailed selling. The no-sayer may be interested in the system's contribution to improved profit. But an even greater interest may be directed to the bells, whistles, and flags of its composition, to the contribution to cost and effectiveness by each component, and to its competitive assets or liabilities. Risk-taking must be minimized in keeping with a no-sayer's value system that emphasizes caution, conformity, cost reduction, a tight control system, and the development of a high level of confidence before finding no reason not to go ahead.

To meet these needs, you may have to engage in exhaustively detailed multiple presentations. Here is a checklist of appeals to no-sayers:

1. Cautious decisionmaking based on fair and full evaluation of measurable facts and figures.
2. Conformity to standard industry practice.
3. Demonstrable cost reduction accomplished by new efficiencies or elimination of old inefficiencies.
4. A tight control system to measure operating cost efficiency and to apply quick remedial action.
5. Confidence acquired from independent evaluation of claims, case histories based on customer testimonials, and personal visits to similar installations that are up and running.

How to Deal with Influencers

Influencers may have either official or political pull that they apply to decisionmakers, often swaying them. Influencers are the most difficult power-wielders to identify. Many of them are obscure. Since their power takes the form of personal influence, they may not hold high titles. In fact, many influencers are technical experts who function at middle organization levels but whose knowledge is called on by yes-sayers in their decisionmaking.

In addition to the power they are given because of their expertise, influencers may hold political power that yes-sayers can use to feel out and manipulate reaction to their decisions. Holders of social power may also be influential in recommending action to yes-sayers.

Finding the hidden sources of influence in an organization is a difficult assignment. Once identified, they must be dealt with individually on the basis of their power. The influencer who holds expert power in technology, finance, or operations must be approached in technical terms with facts and figures from respected sources. Your company's technical support resources can help. So can case histories, customer testimonials, and demonstration visits to similar system installations.

Political and social power-holders must be influenced in terms of their personal values and interpersonal relationships and how the system will affect them. You will also be wise to emphasize how these benefits can be communicated in the most positive manner throughout the organization so that the influencers' images will be enhanced in the eyes of superiors, peers, and the organization at large. No important organization toes can be stepped on. No empires can be invaded or eliminated nor can entrenched power-wielders be displaced. In short, the political and social structure must be preserved.

Here is a checklist of appeals to influencers with a technical power base:

1. Facts and figures to bear out claims attested to by respected independent or third-party sources.
2. Case history documentation.
3. Customer testimonials.
4. Personal visits to similar installations.

Influencers with a political and social power base can be approached according to this checklist:

1. Beneficial effects on interpersonal relations of all people importantly affected, with specific reference to the absence of career threats and maintenance or enhancement of political and official position in the power structure.
2. Aid in communicating benefits throughout the organization and the community at large.

Decisionmaker Partnering

Every decisionmaker can be considered as a fraction. The denominator is always the same: common needs and aspirations. Every numerator, though, is exceptional; numerators are composed of individual differences. In order to penetrate a customer organization, you have to analyze what is individual as well as what is common. This can be done by answering two questions: Who are the decisionmakers I can partner with? Who are the decisionmakers I will have difficulty partnering with?

Decisionmakers Who Make Good Partners

There are six types of decisionmakers who have high partnering potential. Figure 8-3 summarizes their principal characteristics and most probable negotiating modes.

Figure 8-3. High-partnering decisionmakers.

Manager Type	Characteristics	Negotiation Modes
Bureaucrat	Rational, formal, impersonal, disciplined, jealous of rights and prerogatives of office, well versed in organizational politics.	Follows the rules. A stickler for compliance. More concerned with tasks than with people. Logical strategist but can be a nitpicker. Predictable negotiator.
Zealot	Competent loner, impatient, outspoken, a nuisance to bureaucrats, insensitive to others, minimal political skills.	Devoted to the good of the organization. Aggressive and domineering negotiator, blunt and direct. Totally task-oriented.
Executive	Dominant but not domineering, directive but permits freedom, consultative but not participative, sizes up people well but relates only on a surface level, cordial but at arm's length.	Organization-oriented. High task concentration. Assertive negotiator. Adroit strategist, flexible and resourceful.
Integrator	Egalitarian, supportive, participative, excellent interpersonal skills, a born team-builder, a catalyst who is adept at unifying conflicting values.	Shares leadership. Permits freedom of decisions and delegates authority. Welcomes ideas. Open and honest negotiator who seeks win-win relationships.
Gamesman	Fast-moving, flexible, upward-moving, impersonal, risktaker, winning is everything, innovative, opportunistic but ethical, plays the game fairly but will give nothing away.	Wants to win every negotiation. Enjoys competition of ideas, jockeying for position and maneuvers of the mind. Sharp, skilled, and tough negotiator. Can be a win-win strategist.
Autocrat	Paternalistic, patronizing, closed to new ideas that are not invented here, not consultative or participative.	Binds people emotionally. Rules from position of authority. Make pronouncements of policy. A sharp trader who negotiates on a tit-for-tat basis.

The Bureaucrat. Despite negative connotations of the term, it is generally not difficult to partner a bureaucrat. The bureaucrat is rational and systemized; policies, procedures, and rules govern all actions. Although friendships and jealousies abound among bureaucrats, and while politicking may be a favorite indoor sport, the selling climate is impersonal. Things get done systematically but not speedily. Divergent personalities and individual eccentricities are discouraged. The organization's way of doing things must be followed to the letter. Selling to a bureaucracy depends on understanding its traditional nature and cultivating its key decisionmakers. It is almost always a long-term process.

The Zealot. Zealots are organizational loners. Although intensely concerned for their organization's welfare, zealots have an apostolic fervor for pet projects, which they always present as being precisely what the organization needs most. Zealots are usually competent. Other people's ideas, however, go largely ignored. Individual and organizational sensitivities are routinely stepped on. You may find zealots overly demanding and sometimes pests. Zealots negotiate by bludgeoning, although they welcome with open arms anyone who can help them attain their objectives. Zealots can be possessive. Since they tend to divide the world into "friends" and "enemies," you must be wary of becoming unduly identified with zealots and their causes.

The Executive. Executives are professional managers, battle-wise, firm-minded, and strong-willed. They get the most out of people by accurately perceiving their strengths and limitations. Executives set a no-nonsense tempo in their organizations. They are sensitive to people but do not get involved with them emotionally. Negotiating with an executive is a straightforward matter of providing demonstrable benefits. An executive looks for incremental values. If they cannot be perceived, negotiation will most likely end promptly.

The Integrator. Integrators are team-building managers. They are easy to negotiate with. Integrators perceive their role not so much as making decisions as managing the decisionmaking process by consensus and collaboration. The integrator is a catalyst whose job is to create superior task accomplishment, individual growth and success, mutual respect, and cooperation. Since most of the integrator's decisions are group decisions, you must partner not only with integrators but also with their key group members.

The Gamesman. Gamesmen run on fast tracks. Highly analytic, flexible, fast-moving, competitive, sharp, and aggressive, they love playing the game of business. Their preoccupation is with forming and re-forming winning teams. The consultant must become a team member. Like the executive, the gamesman relates without becoming emotionally involved. Wisely risk-taking, innovative, and strategically keen, gamesmen enjoy jockeying and maneuvering. Since gamesmen respect peers who are shrewd and adroit, they will challenge every negotiation skill that you possess. Yet gamesmen negotiate within the rules and will be cooperative as long as they believe they can win.

The Paternalistic Autocrat. Autocrats see their role as all-knowing, somewhat patronizing authority figures who demand personal loyalty from subordinates. Friction and conflict are smoothed over. Autocrats can be kind and considerate, but these traits are likely to vanish instantly if they are antogonized or not offered personal loyalty. On the other hand, if you can be "adopted" by an autocrat, a win-win relationship can develop.

Decisionmakers Who Make Difficult Partners

There are six types of decisionmakers who have low partnering potential. Figure 8-4 summarizes their principal characteristics and most probable negotiating modes.

The Machiavellian. Machiavellians generally do not let ethics enter their negotiations. Although they can be ethical when it suits their purposes, they are cynical about people. Machiavellians depersonalize others. They concentrate on winning regardless of the loss incurred by their adversaries. Emotional considerations mean little. Machiavellians never get emotionally involved while negotiating. They use power, always seeking to augment it, and exploit others when it is necessary. Machiavellians lie plausibly, and they are experts at appearing innocent. They prefer ambiguous and unstructured situations, suspect the motives of others, and have little faith in human nature. Although they resist being influenced, they are superior at influencing. Machiavellians press to get all they can from every relationship. Tradeoffs are a distasteful last resort.

The Missionary. Missionaries are opposite to Machiavellians—wholly concerned with people, their feelings and reactions. Good human relations, harmony, and intimacy are their criteria for negotiation; confrontation and conflict are avoided. Missionaries often win popularity contests but less regularly win respect. Their strategies are almost always interpersonal. Negotiation means reaching agreement or delaying it in a pleasant manner. As a result, you may always be uncertain about when an agreement will be finalized. A negative reaction will be communicated as sweetly as a positive one.

The Exploitive Autocrat. Exploiters are arrogant, harsh, and

Figure 8-4. Low-partnering decisionmakers.

Manager Type	Characteristics	Negotiation Modes
Machiavellian	Self-oriented, shrewd, devious and calculating, insightful into weaknesses of others, opportunistic, suave and charismatic, can turn in instant from collaboration to aggression.	An exploiter of people. Cooperates only for selfish interests. Totally impersonal negotiator, unmoved by human appeals. Will win as inexpensively as possible but will win at all costs.
Missionary	Smoother of conflict, blender of ideas, must be liked, identifies harmony with acceptance, highly subjective and personal.	A seeker of compromise and leveler of ideas to lowest common denominator. Negotiates emotionally with personal appeals to agree for his sake.
Exploiter	Arrogant, what's-in-it-for-me attitude, coercive, domineering, rigid, prejudiced, takes advantage of weakness, makes snap judgments unswayed by evidence.	Exerts constrictive personal control over negotiation. Makes others vulnerable by using pressure and fear to get own way. Demands subservience. Sees others as a obstacles to be overcome.
Climber	Striving, driving, smooth and polished demeanor that masks aggression, opportunistic, without loyalty to others, goes with flow.	Excellent politician. Uses selfpropelling change to call attention to himself. Always thinking ahead. Self-serving negotiator based on what-will-this-do-for-me?
Conserver	Defends status quo, resists change, favors evolutionary improvement, uses the system skillfully to safeguard personal position and prerogatives.	Imposes own sense of order and nonimmediacy on negotiation. Slows everything down. Preaches traditional values. Defensively blocks innovation and undermines agreements before implementation.
Glad-Hander	Superficially friendly to new ideas but essentially a nondoer, effusive, socially skilled and politically skillful, superior survival instincts.	Overreactive and overstimulated by everything but impressed by little. Promises support but then fades away. Endorses only sure things that can do some personal good. Never takes risks.

vengeful. They demand subservience. Ruling by threats and fear, exploiters assume that consultants are incompetent and must be driven to do an acceptable job. This is McGregor's Theory X manager, distrustful of people in the extreme. Negotiating with exploiters is difficult. You must be ready to encounter exploiters on their own terms: strength for strength, force for force.

The Climber. Climbers ceaselessly seek opportunities for self-advancement. Their loyalty, like that of Machiavellians, is to themselves. They use negotiating situations to propel themselves toward power and status. Climbers use aggressive strategies against the weak, and defensive strategies against those who attempt to constrain them. When blocked, climbers move laterally. Whereas a Machiavellian may be content to be the power behind a throne, climbers insist on being front and center. You must be wary lest climbers use you. Climbers can also help you, but identification with a climber may invite hostility, particularly from other climbers.

The Conserver. Conservers are hoarding types. They are basically stand-patters and status quo defenders. Anything new disturbs a conserver. Since they have usually gone as far as they are likely to go, conservers are generally jealous of whatever prerogatives they possess. In contrast to the Machiavellian, the climber, and the exploiter, who can become a consultant's helpers and recommenders, conservers are almost always hinderers. They safeguard their positions by throwing obstacles in your way. Sabotage of innovative change is their forte.

The Glad-Hander. Glad-handers are marketing personalities. Sociable, infinitely adaptable, extroverted, and superficially friendly, glad-handers are unprincipled. They are incapable of lasting loyalty. They are salable commodities, up for hire to the highest bidder. Yet they are charming and personable, possessing high social skills. You may be taken in at first by glad-handers because of their polished social veneer. But glad-handers do not wear well, especially under pressure. Partnering with glad-handers is a futile endeavor, but they can often be helpful in running interference to reach decisionmakers.

9

How to Ensure Partnerable Rewards

You and your support staff are the essential partnering agents in Consultative Selling. Together, you compose a profit improvement team for each of your customers. You, the consultant, are the leader of the team. You will partner with the customer business function managers whose costs you can reduce and with the managers of the customer's lines of business whose sales can be increased. The minimal resources you need as team leader, and their relationship to you, are shown in Figure 9-1.

Three types of support from within your company will be essential: financial, data, and technical. All supportive team members will play two roles. Internally, within the team, they will coach and counsel you in preparing and presenting Profit Improvement Proposals, as well as implementing them. Externally, they will create partnerships with their correlates in the customer's business—finance to finance, data to data, technical to technical.

Your first act as consultant should be to form your profit improvement team on a customer-by-customer basis. Your second act is to consult with your customers on the organization of companion teams composed of their own staff support resources. As Figure 9-2 shows, a customer team is built around the decisionmakers who will be your partners. By melding the two teams, you create your partnership.

You have the right to expect the customer team to acknowledge two responsibilities: to share access with you and your team and to

Figure 9-1. Consultative profit improvement team.

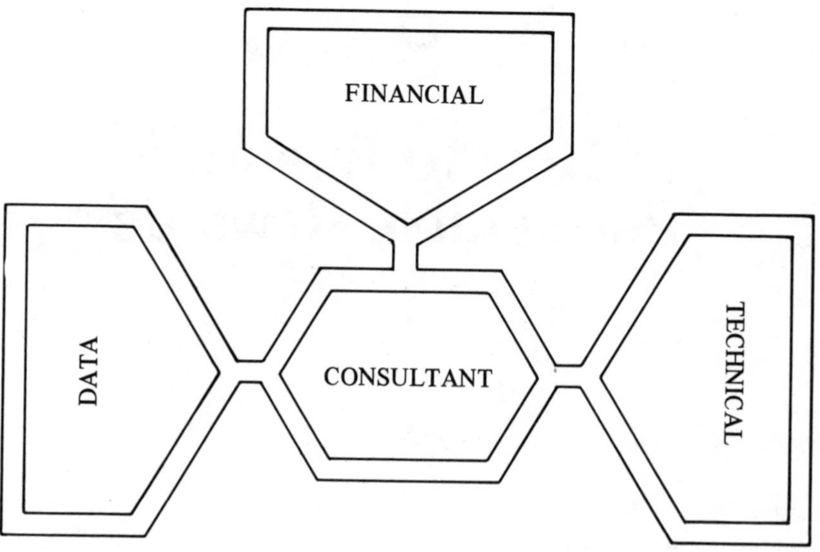

Figure 9-2. Customer profit improvement team.

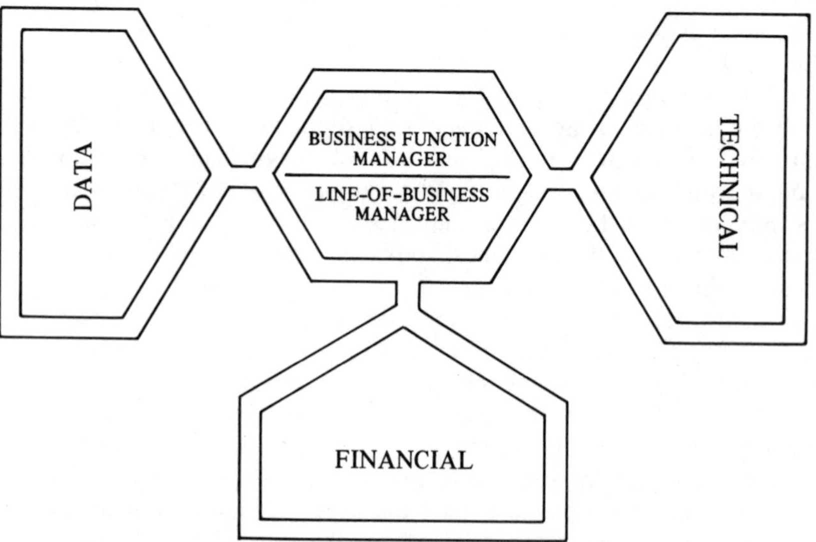

share data. The customer team has rights as well. They are known as the rights of partnership:

1. *"Cure me."* Get things done, respond to my needs. Produce results fast because I have more needs.
2. *"Talk my language."* Speak to me in profit improvement language. Show me that you identify with me and that you know my business.
3. *"Don't surprise me."* Install a control system so I can be comfortable. Let me share in evaluating our work together.
4. *"Level with me."* Tell it like it is. Criticize constructively. Tell me what's wrong, but let me know what's right, too.
5. *"Get into my business."* Become a part of my team. Be around, ask questions. Don't be disruptive.
6. *"Be reasonable."* Give a premium value in return for your premium price; superior profit makes price justifiable.
7. *"Be competent."* Give me the best you have. Be a real professional.
8. *"Teach me."* While you sell or perform, teach me how. Share your experience and expertise with me and my people.
9. *"Take leadership."* Get out in front of my problems. Roll up your sleeves and get your hands dirty in my operations.
10. *"Worry for me."* Think hard about my problems. Let me know what you think even without my asking. Give me immediate access to you when I am worried; be available. Put my needs first.
11. *"Innovate."* Give me something that's better than you give anyone else. Make me preeminent; make me stand out. Apply yourself in a way that transcends normal boundaries. Offer me options.
12. *"Be faithful."* Keep our business confidential. Make your relationship with me personal; don't pass me along to others.
13. *"Be motivated."* Show desire to achieve our objectives. Be genuinely interested in my problems. Don't leave a single stone unturned in looking for solutions.
14. *"Be flexible."* Compromise with me once in a while but don't give in on what you know is vital.
15. *"Treat me like a person, not just a client."* Treat me like an equal; deal with me one to one. Don't talk down to me. Throw in a few little extras every now and then. Advise me on closely related matters even if you're not being paid for them.

Once the profit improvement teams begin to achieve results together, the major reward from partnering can occur: partners tend to shut out competitors for each other's time, information, and resources. Partners tend to exclude the attempts of third parties to partner, so that departnering is made less likely. But it remains a threat nonetheless.

Preventing Departnering

Departnering occurs when two conditions are met. An alliance that is incomplete or unfulfilled within itself is vulnerable. Then, when a more promising partner appears, it succumbs. Many troubled partnerships linger on because both partners temporarily subscribe to the belief that "You know what you've got, but you don't know what you're going to get." As soon as one partner believes that what he or she is going to get is better, the partnership will end. In Consultative Selling, this means that the customer will also be lost.

Because markets are tight communities, the loss of one key customer inevitably raises doubts, creates assumptions, and fosters anxieties that threaten the stability of other key customer relations. A domino effect can follow. The loss of one key account opens the door to competitors who, even if they have not been a cause of departnering, will be anxious to take advantage of its effects.

What leaves a partnership incomplete or causes it to be unfulfilled? There are two major factors that predispose to eventual departnering: divergence of objective and inequality of risk.

1. *Divergent objective*. Partnerships rest on a common objective. Both partners must have the same result in mind before they partner, see the same result as being achieved while they are partnering, and be able to look back at the accomplishment of their result as a consequence of the partnership.

Consultative partnerships are known by the objective the partners have in common. The eternal question of what partners see in each other is easily answered: They want to achieve the same objective and they perceive the partnership as the optimal means of reaching it. This is their hidden agenda.

A consultative partnership is not a one-on-one situation. More accurately, it is a two-for-one relationship. Both partners share one objective—to improve the customer's profit. Unless this is accomplished, the consultant's objective of improving profit on sales will be impossible. For this reason, the customer's objective must come first for both of them. It is not philanthropy but enlightened self-interest that makes it so.

When objectives diverge, or simply appear to be going off in different directions or losing conviction, alliances atomize. A customer partner may acquire the belief that the consultant is more interested in self-promotion to the customer's top tier than in merchandising the partnership. The customer partner may feel used, demeaned, and taken unfair advantage of by helping the consultant develop business elsewhere, either inside or outside the organization. The consultant, on the other hand, may believe many of the same things about the customer partner. Whether such perceptions are true or not, they will have an erosive effect on the partnership.

Restating objectives and recommitting to them are essential elements in keeping partnerships on track. Objectives should be brought up for discussion at frequent intervals; this should be at the consultant's initiative. A good time to introduce them is when progress is being measured against them. At some of these checkpoints, the original objective may have to be downgraded. Perhaps it can be increased. In either event, keeping objectives current will perpetuate the values that both partners are working for.

2. *Unequal risk.* Partnerships are a means of reducing risk. Two parties can share the load, divide the responsibility, and parcel out the components of the risk that would otherwise be borne by one or left undone. Although risk can be reduced, it can never be eliminated. It must be shared as equally as possible if the partnership is to be preserved. Otherwise, one partner may accuse the other of "putting your hand out farther than your neck."

No matter how hard consultants try to bring into balance the risks inherent in improving customer profits, customers will always be left with the major exposure. They are exposed on their own behalf. They are exposed on their recommendation of the consultant. And they are exposed to their topmost tier of management. In any business situation, there can be no riskier combination of exposures.

Once customers commit themselves to work with a consultant to improve their profit, they must be successful. It is no wonder that they will be ultrasensitive to their own inherent risk and to the support they receive from you. They have a lot on the line.

Because customers bear the major share of partnership risk, you must take on the major share of reducing the risk and providing the reassurance that it has been reduced. There is no way you can have the same degree of risk as your customers, but you can provide a greater degree of risk calculation and limitation. This must be your equalizer.

In Consultative Selling, you have several equalizing tools at your disposal. One is to be thorough in your fact-finding and in putting together your database on customer problems and opportunities. Another is to be diligent in obtaining feedback from your customers about their needs. A third is to manage your progress review sessions with care so that deviations from objectives are caught early and corrected, so that strategies can be revised to meet changed conditions, and so that opportunities can be capitalized when they are still fully available.

If you fail to keep a partnership's objective unified or its risks from being equalized, the result is fairly easy to forecast. Your customer will seek a new partner who meets two qualifications: a lowered risk and a more harmonious objective. In the process, the customer may find a partner who can deliver higher objectives. These may come in the form of greater profits, a more optimal mix, or a broader range of options to choose from. Improved objectives may also come from a quicker flow of profits, with new monies coming on stream sooner or existing costs being reduced faster.

When objectives fall out of harmony, and the inequality of risk becomes uncomfortably oppressive, the emergence of a new partner is inevitable. It invariably is a lengthy process for customers to decide to open up a search, evaluate candidates, and then hold their breath while they make a selection. But it always seems sudden to the consultants on whom the boom is lowered. Their lack of awareness is the proof of the pudding about how far the partners have drifted apart.

The history of terminated partnerships is filled with surprised consultants. "Why, it was only yesterday" they say, "that he was telling me what a great guy I was—how much we had been through together and how he would always be indebted to me." If it was not "only yesterday," it was "only last week" or "last month." The epitaph is generally the same: How great it *was*. Meanwhile, for the new partner, the benediction is: How great it is *going to be*.

Migrating Initial Sales

Key account penetration through Consultative Selling is a reciprocal process. Preliminary partnering makes possible initial entry at top tier levels. Once entry has been accomplished, partnering should proceed apace so that migration opportunities open up beyond the initial sale. The purpose of preliminary partnering is to gain entry. The purpose of entry is to migrate, to penetrate a customer business in ever-expanding breadth and depth from your breakthrough point. The purpose of migration is to grow the customer's business and your business again and again.

In addition to the obvious benefit of providing ongoing high-margin sales opportunities, migration offers several other advantages. It helps amortize the investment in data collection. It helps develop new information sources about a customer business. It spreads awareness of your consultative positioning. And it helps deny opportunistic chances for competition to move in on a problem that you can, and should, solve. It helps prevent departnering.

Some migrations occur naturally—the solution of one problem leads progressively to the discovery of another, or a solution in one division stimulates customer interest about its transfer to a similar problem in another division. Other migrations will take place only as a result of effort. You will have to search out opportunities in the nooks and crannies of your customer businesses, relying on your partners to coach you about the most productive areas to explore and to point out the most cooperative guides to ask for advice.

The objective of penetrating a customer business in depth is to serve all major needs with your major products, services, or systems. This concept can be called maximizing "share of customer" as long as it is understood that it is not simply a volume criterion—it is a standard of the importance of your involvement. If you are significantly involved, you can become the preferred supplier of your customers' improved profits. Penetration in depth is inextricably tied to penetration in important areas of a business. Migration must be a selective policy whose aim is to consolidate your position as profit-improver of the most vital functions you can affect.

The ideal migration timetable makes improving profit in one function the jumping-off place for improving profit in the next function. In this way, you can extract maximum learning value from each experience. You can also avoid stretching your resources too thin across more assignments than you can handle. It pays to remember that migration works both ways. One significant success encourages permission to try another. One significant failure discourages permission to try anything more at all.

Installing an initial system should therefore be regarded as planting the seed for follow-on sales opportunities, not the end of the sale. Once a sale has been made, the consultant has acquired a major asset: a more profitable customer. You can benefit the customer even further by additional profit improvement through one or more of three types of migration. You can offer to *supplement* the initial system with added components. Perhaps some components may have been sacrificed for financial reasons at the time the original system was approved. Or perhaps a greater need has become apparent only after installation. As a second type of followup, you can offer to *upgrade* the original components, up to and including the ultimate upgrading, which is total replacement of the system. Or third, you can offer to *integrate* an entirely new complementary system with the initial system.

These profit improvement opportunities are not mutually exclusive. You can use all three approaches in sequence with the same customer. First, you can supplement the entry system. Then, at a later date, you can upgrade some of the original components. Finally, a complementary new system can be integrated with the original one. Then you can recycle the sales approach by offering to supplement the new system, then upgrade it, and eventually integrate a third system with the first two.

This recycling strategy is illustrated by the following scenario. It begins *after* an initial system is in place and producing prescribed profit improvement benefits.

Cycle 1

1. Supplement initial system with add-on components.
2. Upgrade components of initial system with technically innovated products or equipment.
3. Integrate a complementary new system with the initial system.

Cycle 2

1. Supplement new system with add-on components.
2. Upgrade components of new system with technically innovated products or equipment.
3. Integrate a second complementary system with one or the other existing system.

Cycle 3

Repeat Cycle 2.

Supplementing an Original System

Many systems are sold lean. They are constructed of only minimum components, or every individual component offers just the minimum performance required, or both. It is often easier for the consultant to sell a minimal entry system. Such a foot-in-the-door sale may have its greatest value in migration opportunity for follow-on sales.

Upgrading Original Components

The consultant's technology-support capability is a major sales point. Customers expect to become its beneficiaries. It is also one of the consultant's major cost components. For both reasons, the consultant must pay off on technical capability by upgrading a system's original components on a progressive, periodic basis. The ultimate upgrading, of course, is the replacement of an entire system by an upgraded one.

Technological innovation almost always raises the cost of a system. Accordingly, it must also raise the consultant's ability to improve customer profit. If customers have a leasing agreement, they may be able to incorporate newly improved products and equipment into their system without an additional fee. When customers have a purchase agreement, tradeins of original equipment can make it easy for them to obtain upgraded components.

Free modifications with upgraded components can create customer good will. They may also encourage a customer to make increased use of a system's equipment in order to derive the benefits of faster, better performance. If a system uses consumables, their use will increase also. In addition to improving revenues, upgrading may also generate important cost reduction benefits. Costly service calls and repairs can be greatly reduced once upgraded equipment is installed. In these ways, the annual return on conversion cost can be 50 percent or higher.

Integrating a Complementary System

Systems are designed to improve the profit of a specific business function. Once a system begins to deliver its benefits, the potential for achieving similar benefits in closely related or interacting functions may become apparent. In such a case, the consultant is in an excellent position to recommend a complementary new system that can be integrated with the customer's initial system.

You must be careful to sell the new system on its own merits as a profit-improver. This means that the new system's specific contribution to profit and cost should be carefully spelled out, along with its service requirements and operating peculiarities. If it cannot stand on its own in this way, it should not be recommended. The reason for this caution is simple to explain: It is based on the double-or-nothing principle.

Although it is true that the best customer for a new system is an existing customer, the consultant can just as easily lose two sales as make two. If the second system fails to deliver the promised benefits, both systems are at risk. The second system's problems will almost inevitably contaminate customer perception of the original system. Even though the initial system continues to deliver improved profit, its most vital component—the consultant's personal expertise—will come into question.

Ensuring Customer Continuity

The ultimate criterion of partnership is that neither partner can afford to let the other partner go. Each is too valuable. Each represents too much profit potential. Each embodies too much of an investment that promises yet unrealized results.

Partners in a consultative alliance are priceless assets, impossible to replicate. Their loss is the equivalent of a catastrophic failure. It is unthinkable.

This kind of customer continuity can be ensured only by your ability to apply customer knowledge. In the last analysis, it is who you know among top tier customer decisionmakers and how much you know about their business operations that gives you insurance against departnering. Your interpersonal abilities to penetrate top tier customer management and the integrity of your customer database are the two principal assets in creating and extending consultative relationships. Given these, you can put your profit improvement skills to work.

How can you become this sort of partner and nail down the continuity of your key customer alliances? The following scenario provides the answer. It is taken from an actual dialog between a well-partnered customer and a would-be usurper of the consultant partner's role.

"I would like to work with you in the privileged position that Phil Smith of the Continental Group now enjoys."

"Phil privileges us. That is why he is privileged."

"Exactly what does he do for you that privileges you so much?"

"Phil helps us improve our profit more than we can improve it without him . . . more than we can improve it ourselves . . . more than we can improve it with anyone else in the functions of our business that he affects."

"I can affect those same functions. Our companies, his and mine, are directly competitive. I may be able to improve your profit every bit as much as he does."

"But he already *is*. The best you can say is that you *may*."

"How can I say I can unless you let me try?"

"I can't let you try until I know you can."

"Then how did Phil Smith ever get started with you if he had to prove he could improve your profit before you let him?"

"That's how. He showed us how much profit he could improve. It was only then that we let him."

"I would like to show you how much profit I could improve. Then you would have a choice: Smith's company or mine."

"You said you might be able to improve our profit as much as Phil Smith does. Even if you could, how could we choose you? In order for us to consider replacing Phil, you would have to do better than he does for us . . . not just the same."

"How would it be if for every dollar of improved profit that Smith gets for you, I can give you an extra ten cents?"

"That might not be enough to justify making a change even if you could do it. And you realize that doing it once wouldn't be enough. You'd have to do it consistently. Otherwise, we'd be better off with Phil."

"Well, how much better would be enough for you?"

"Before we could switch from Phil Smith with comfort and conviction, we'd probably have to have someone give us between fifty percent and a hundred percent more profit. And again, it would have to be consistently."

"All right. Suppose I can do that?"

"How would you go about it?"

"Because we want your business, we'd work harder. We'd be better motivated. We'd work smarter, too. We'd put our best brains against your problems. Besides, we have a better product. Your results would have to be better."

"But fifty percent to a hundred percent better? That's a lot. Even Phil Smith hasn't been able to do that for us."

"That's the best reason in the world for you to switch."

"It may be the worst reason. It may be that Phil knows something that you don't know."

"What's that?"

"Our company. Our business. Our people. Our operating constraints. In one word—us."

Appendix A: Rebranding Strategy for Consultative Selling of Mature Products

At the top tier level of a key account's management, you must sell results. There is no choice—only results will be bought. Results are easiest to establish with a product or service that can produce a demonstrably unique operating and financial result in the customer's business: a *brand*. Because a brand can deliver a premium result, a premium price can be demanded in return.

Mature products have usually lost their ability to contribute premium results to a customer. They contribute parity results, benefits similar to those that their competitors can supply. This similarly certifies their status as commodities. Since key account sales depend so heavily on premium results, mature products may have to be *rebranded;* that is, rejuvenated with a brand's capabilitity for providing superior operating and financial benefits.

A commodity may be rebranded in two ways. One is by going back to the drawing board for technological revamping. The other is by marketing renovation. The decision is not either/or. Companies that choose technological change will still have to incorporate new marketing strategies alongside their new engineering.

Making Changes to Rebrand

There are four principal changes to be made before rebranding can take place:

1. *Profit improvement needs analysis*. You will have to learn customer and industry norms for the business functions you affect. What

are cost norms: for sales, for product development, for manufacturing, for inventory, for distribution—and how does your customer compare? What are profit norms on sales? Is your customer above or below them? What is the norm for collection time on receivables, and how far above the norm is your customer? How much money is the customer leaving on the table as a result every year?

2. *Profit improvement contribution analysis*. You will have to learn the impact you make on customer business, either by backtracking on previous applications of your product line to customer business functions or by monitoring the effects of prototype installations. By using these techniques, you can determine each system's ability to lower a function's cost or raise its sales revenues. This capability will then have to be translated in terms of average profit dollars and average percentage rates of return on investment. These averages will provide ballpark guidelines for the specific values you can predict for each function's improved profit contribution within each customer account.

3. *Systems protection*. You may have to add value to your product by packaging it into a system that will surround it with complementary products and services that can be sold as a single cost-reducing or sales-increasing unit. The system's combined price can then be presented as an investment. Its profit improvement capability can be shown as return on the investment.

4. *Consultative Selling*. The key account sales force will have to be trained to sell the system's rate of return to customers—not the product and service system that produces it or the mature product that has been incorporated into the system.

The essential difference between Consultative Selling of a rebranded product or system and vendor selling of commodity products can be dramatized in this way:

A product-driven commodity sales representative in the chemicals business sells "pounds" to customers by saying: "Our product will solve your formulation problem. It is safe, effective, high in quality, in good supply, and available at competitive prices. We provide free application services to help you ensure the solution."

A consultative representative in the same industry makes a very different approach, even though the product is completely undifferentiated: "The annual cost contributed by your formulation functions can be reduced by $50,000. In return for a one-time $100,000 investment, you can expect a first-year saving of $50,000 and an annual saving thereafter of $50,000. This gives you payback in two years and adds $50,000 to your profit every year for as long as your formulation process remains the same."

In the first instance, a mature product is being sold on its comparative technical specifications and the performance benefits that can be derived from them. Since competition has matched them, one of two things must happen. Either increasingly finite distinctions must be painstakingly explained by the representative, raising the cost of every sale, or the price must be progressively lowered, reducing the representative's margins. Either way, profit from sales is reduced.

In the second instance, the customer's investment and the amount and flow of the return it will yield are being used as the basis for a purchase decision. The product remains a commodity. But when its benefits are rebranded, it can be sold at a premium price.

Rebranding One of the World's Largest Companies

In the late 1960s, AT&T was catapulated by legislative fiat from a monopolistic utility into the competitive marketplace. In common with most utilities, AT&T's strength had been in providing reactive service, not in campaigning for aggressive sales. Its market knowledge was weak. It knew its customers in terms of their peculiar arrays of wiring installations, but not as businesses with problems that could be solved by the application of telecommunications technology. It was organized along operating lines, not according to markets. Its monopoly position had allowed the company to control the rate of obsolescence for its products and to commercialize new technology as management—not the market—decreed. As a result, the majority of its outstanding hardware was composed of mature products.

Within a short period of time, this mature inventory was in key account competition with IBM, ITT, and GTE as well as with young, dynamic marketers whose technology was much more responsive to market needs and whose prices were lower. Under this type of pincers attack, AT&T turned to three strategies to preserve, and to grow, the commercial and industrial business sector of its multibillion-dollar annual revenue stream.

1. *Industry-need specialization.* As a utility, AT&T had segmented its markets according to customer size: small general businesses or major corporate and government users. Markets were resegmented on the basis of industry needs to use telecommunications technology for reducing operating costs or for increasing sales revenues. In each segment, the single most important growth resource was the AT&T industry information base on where customer costs could be reduced and how customer sales revenues could be improved.

2. *Industry-by-industry positioning*. By applying its knowledge of industry costs and sales opportunities that can be affected by telecommunications, AT&T positioned itself as each industry's preferred "profit-improving problem-solver." The company's main approach to customers was financial. The problems for which it prescribed, installed, and monitored solutions were considered solved only when customer profits had been improved.

Key account managers and their marketing, technical, and information teams were taught to carry out a three-step sales procedure with customers: (1) identify a problem and quantify its negative effect; (2) quantify the positive effect of the most cost-effective system to solve the problem; (3) sell the dollars-and-cents effect as representing the value added by AT&T. A simplified case story will illustrate the Consultative Selling approach.

A typical problem that can be solved by telecommunications technology is a sluggish accounts receivable process that deprives access to cash flow. For one customer, AT&T discovered that four separate functions—billing, accounting, sales, and legal—were involved in past-due collections. Twenty-two separate steps, each adding costs, were necessary to collect many receivables. Others were never collected. The average annual earnings loss on receivables outstanding more than 30 days was $1.75 million. This was the customer's true cost of its collection system.

To solve the problem, AT&T prescribed a telemarketing collection system. The customer's annual investment was about $350,000. The net annual saving to the customer was $1.4 million, all of which could be brought down to the bottom line as the increased annual profit contributed by AT&T.

3. *Return-on-investment sales consultation*. AT&T consulted on the improvement of its customers' profit, not simply supplying them with hardware and technological knowhow. Customers were no longer asked to spend money, incur costs, or lease equipment. Instead, sales presentations adopted the style of financial plans that document a positive return on the customer's investment. An AT&T system became valued by a customer according to the return on investment it delivered, not the cost of the products from which it had been assembled.

Appendix B: Marketcentering Strategy for Consultative Selling to Dedicated Markets

There is no substitute for market dedication as the source of profit growth from sales. Market dedication means focusing resources on specific markets that are the core of profit contribution. The best way to accomplish this resource focus is to build it into the organizational structure of the business, so that major markets become the centers around which key account sales take place.

Companies that adopt top tier selling as a way of life are increasingly organizing around key markets instead of around their product or processing capabilities.

IBM organizes its operations according to its key markets, such as institutions like hospitals and retail establishments like supermarkets. Xerox Information Systems Group, which sells copiers and duplicators, converted from geographical selling to vertical selling by industry. Even the strict technical-processing orientation of some scientific companies is giving way to a combined product and market orientation. In its electronics product marketing, Hewlett-Packard has created a sales and service group that concentrates separately on the electrical manufacturing market, while another group serves the market for aerospace. Still other groups concentrate their sales exclusively on the markets for communications or transportation equipment.

General Electric has constructed marketcentered business groups for its major appliance and power-generation businesses. For GE, the process of reorganizing from a product to a market orientation has been especially difficult. An average department used to contain three and one-half product lines and served more than one business or, more frequently, only a part of a major business. Electric motors, for example, were once divided among eight departments. Home refrigerators were split between two departments, even though the only significant product difference was the way the doors open. In such a setup, department managers understandably became oriented to specific product lines rather than to the needs of a total market.

In other companies, a wide range of businesses are being centered on their markets. At Mead, broad market clusters serve customer needs in building and furnishing homes, as well as in education and leisure. Monsanto has organized a Fire Safety Center that consolidates fire-protection products from every sector of the company and groups them according to the market they serve: building and construction, transportation, apparel, or furnishings. Revlon has been engaged in "breaking up the company into little pieces": Six autonomous profit centers are each designed to serve a specific market segment.

PPG Industries has been examining the benefits of systemizing the sales of its paint, ceramics, and glass divisions through a Home Environment Center. The Center's product mix could look like this:

Interior Protection and Performance Group

Glass doors.
Ceramic kitchen countertops and work surfaces.
Interior household paints.

Exterior Protection and Performance Group

Glass doors, windows, and window walls.
Ceramic poolside and picnic areas.
Exterior household paints.

By making a market the center of a sales organization's focus—instead of a product, a process, or a region—banks have been serving the common financial needs of manufacturers of electronics systems with a dedicated key account sales force. Another separate sales force calls on drug and cosmetics accounts. Still another sells financial sources to household product makers.

Benefits of Marketcentering

Defining a business according to its key customer markets by organizing to serve comprehensive sets of their needs with dedicated sales groups can produce several major benefits:

1. A marketcenter forms a natural supply center. The sales and distribution of all the products and services that can be used by the same market are centralized with a single sales organization.

2. A marketcenter ensures that customers will be required to deal only with a single representative to gain access to the sum total of a supplier's product lines and services.

3. A marketcenter permits key account sales representatives and their support teams who are dedicated to a single industry to become unusually well versed in its people, problems, and the customer processes into which they must sell.

4. A marketcenter provides a ready-made environment for an APACHE industry database on its problems and opportunities.

5. A marketcenter allows its customers to identify the market-centered supplier as the premier source of supply that specializes in solving their unique problems.

Guidelines for Marketcentering

If key account sales are currently centered around one or more product lines, around the manufacturing processes that make them, or around geographical territories, three guidelines will help a conversion to marketcentering.

First, a marketcenter must be chartered to serve a market that is defined according to closely related needs. This permits the market to be served by a diversified system of products and services that, taken together, supply a combination of closely related benefits. The marketcenter may sell two or more related products in a single sale or sell a system composed of products and their related services.

Second, because a marketcenter is operated as a profit center, it should be administered by a business manager. Unlike product managers or brand managers, or even market managers who are merely profit-accountable, business managers are responsible for both profit and volume. They enjoy considerable authority in running their businesses. They command the key decisions. They set prices, control costs, and are charged with operating their marketcenter for a satisfactory profit on sales.

Finally, once a key account sales group is marketcentered, its storehouse of market information becomes its key asset. Through marketcentering, an industry information center can be set up to store and give broad industrywide access to its market knowledge on a fee basis.

Two case histories will illustrate how these guidelines have been implemented by two very different corporations, NCR and General Foods, to achieve a similar objective: enable a single sales representative to serve all or most of each key customer's needs in the industry of the representative's dedication.

The NCR Approach

NCR organized its traditional product-line sales approach into a strategy of "selling by vocation" on an industry-by-industry basis. Each vocation is a broad industry grouping that forms a specific market definable by reasonably cohesive needs. NCR concentrates a separate sales force on each of the following vocational markets: financial institutions, retailers, commercial and industrial businesses, and computer customers in medical, educational, and government offices.

NCR's marketcentered sales organization enables it to be more competitive, especially in the marketing of systems. In each market, the NCR key account sales representative assigned to it can sell coordinated systems of numerical recording and sorting products. Previously, each sales representative could sell only one divisional or departmental product line. As a result, a customer decisionmaker could be simultaneously involved with several NCR sales representatives. No one of them could possibly know the sum total of the customer's numerical control needs, let alone be able to serve them. Under the marketcentered approach, the same retail industry sales representative who sells an NCR cash register to a department store can also search out and serve the store's needs for NCR accounting machines, data entry terminals, and a mainframe computer. If the representative needs help, he or she can organize a team with other NCR representatives that can bring the required strength to a proposal. The product groups that the representative sells are still manufactured separately. The sales approach centered on markets is the innovation that makes the difference.

By selling systems of products through a single sales representative or sales team, rather than selling individual products through many uncoordinated representatives, NCR is helping its key customers achieve greater profit improvement. It can prescribe systems to solve comprehensive problems that would otherwise remain immune to single-product solutions. Sales management also believes it can expand its profitable sales volume by selling larger packages and insulating its position against competition.

Each vocational marketcenter's full range of recording and sorting needs is becoming better known to NCR. In turn, by specializing in seeking out and serving these needs, each of NCR's vocational sales organizations is becoming known for expertise in its market, almost as if it were an independent specialist company. Moreover, every sales group can utilize the total financial and technical resources of the company for professional counsel and support in developing, prescribing, and installing product systems.

The General Foods Approach

Whereas NCR was motivated to marketcenter by the increasing preferences of its customers for systems and by the relentless competitive pressures of IBM, General Foods revised its approach because of internal strains and frustrations. New product winners had either stopped coming out of product development at their former rate or carried an unreasonable cost. Better knowledge of the needs of its consumers was obviously required if the company's product developers were to harmonize their technologies with the new lifestyles influencing the demand for processed foods. At the same time, the needs of the company's customers at the retail level required new responses. Competitive brands were proliferating, clamoring for shelf and display space. An increasingly attractive profit on sales was making private-label products more acceptable to major supermarket chains.

These events combined to place unprecedented strains on the company's divisional structure, which was the legacy of a generations-old policy of acquisition. General Foods' major food divisions—Birds-Eye, Jell-O, Post, and Kool-Aid—had evolved historically, each according to the process technology that it brought into the company. As the scope of each division's product categories grew, it was inevitable that one division's consumer provinces would be impinged on by other divisions. As a result, each market was served in a fragmented rather than a concentrated manner. Divisional sovereignties frequently made it impossible for the company to dominate a market that was served by two or more divisions with related product categories but with different styles and degrees of commitment.

Often more damaging for new product development was the way in which division managers respected a no-man's-land between their provinces. This left gaps in product categories that gave competitors a clear shot. Even when they missed, the gaps prevented General Foods from establishing a position of undeniable category leadership.

The General Foods approach to marketcentering reorganized its process-oriented division structure into separate selling organizations. Each marketcenter concentrates on selling families of products made by different processing technologies but consumed by the same market segment. The Dessert Food Center, for example, coordinates the sales strategy for all desserts, whether they are frozen, powdered, or ready-to-eat from three different processing technologies. The Pet Food Center sells dog foods, regardless of whether they come from freeze-dried, dry pellet, or semimoist processes.

Dessert Food Center

Powdered mixes
Frozen
Canned ready-to-eat

Breakfast Food Center

Powdered beverage mixes
Frozen
Canned ready-made

Pet Food Center

Dry pellet
Semimoist
Freeze-dried

This approach of centering entire product families on a market relates the sales organization closely to the needs of the company's retail customers and end-user consumers. Each marketcenter functions like a miniature division. It draws on the full range of corporate technologies and support services such as market research, production, and new product development. Its primary mission is to capture its market by concentrating the corporation's complete range of resources against it.

Two-Way Growth Opportunity

Marketcentering ranks in importance with Alfred Sloan's decentralization of General Motors along market-segmented lines. Market-centered companies regain a customer focus that often became blurred by imitators of Procter & Gamble's brand management system. While contemporary with Sloan's market awareness, brand management directed the styles of many corporate formats away from customers and toward products. When product and brand management were imposed on the traditional manufacturing division and on the pyramid type of organization, which was adapted for the needs of commercial business from Von Moltke's military general staff concept, progress toward marketcentering slowed for half a century.

The beginning of a new thrust toward the customer was first signaled by the advent of free-form marketing groups. They were allowed to cut across corporate pyramids whenever unusual market sensitivity was demanded in an operation. A variety of problem-solving task forces and project management teams came into being for much the same reason; they represented jerry-built improvisations to defeat a product-oriented or process-centered organizational system.

Marketcentering a business can give it a two-way flexibility. Each of its major markets can be sold to more intensively once it is established as the center of a business. The same market can be sold to more extensively as well. Its related needs can be sought out and served along with its primary needs.

Appendix C: Financial Strategy for Consultative Selling of Capital-Intensive Systems

Throughout business, there is an established method used by almost all customers to plan and evaluate their capital expenditures: what they should buy, when they should buy it, and what other options they should consider for investing their funds. The method is known as the capital budgeting process. This process contains four steps: (1) project planning, (2) evaluation and decision making, (3) control and audit of cash commitments, (4) post-audit evaluating and reporting of results.

The first step in capital budgeting proceeds on the assumption that a company has a formal long-range plan or, at the least, the proposed project fits into the mainstream of the corporation's interest. Implicit in a proposal is a forecast of markets, revenues, costs, expenses, profit. These aspects of capital budgeting are the most important, most time-consuming, most critical phase, and largely outside of the area of expertise of the financial executive. A major project generally affects marketing, engineering, manufacturing, and finance.

The uncertainties surrounding a long-range forecast are often great enough to throw doubt on the effectiveness of the entire decision-making process. Probability analysis of success/failure becomes important in view of the uncertainties. A relatively simple approach to evaluating uncertainty is discussed later. However, sophisticated probability analysis and computer simulation can be beneficial in giving credibility to major long-range projections in the face of great uncertainty. Unless

Adapted from "The Capital Budgeting Process," originally published as a monograph by Coopers & Lybrand, 1973, and reprinted by permission. Content and commentary have been contributed by Mack Hanan and J. P. Donis.

this phase of capital budgeting is made reliable and meaningful, the decisionmaking phase simply becomes an exercise in arithmetic.

The second stage, project evaluation and decisionmaking methods, has received major attention in accounting and financial publications. There is general agreement that the time-adjusted cash flow methods (net present value and discounted cash flow [DCF] rate of return) are most meaningful guides to the investment decision; however, there is still place for cash payback analysis in appraising the financial risks inherent in a projection. These methods will be examined and brought into perspective for use in the proposed model. Within certain limits, and they can be identified, these measures will give the best tools for appraising proposals. They do not produce the magic go, no-go answer. They give management guidance. No matter what quantitative guidelines are developed, qualitative factors will be important in the final decision—the personal judgments and preferences of the project sponsor and management cannot be discounted.

The third step, control and audit of cash, is the simplest step in the budgeting process once the source of funds has been determined and committed. After approval, the project should be treated as any other budgeted item, with payment schedules determined and variances reported and explained. Major overspending can impair the validity of the investment decision, and even invalidate the entire process.

A caution is appropriate at this point. When a proposal calls for a specific investment it is implicit that no more than that amount will be spent. Overspending of any significant amount cannot be permitted. Similarly, a project sponsor should not come back the next year for additional funds because he underestimated his original request. When either of these events occurs, it becomes necessary to refigure the entire project on the total cash outlay. Unfortunately, at this point the firm is already irrevocably committed to the project and the new calculations are after the fact.

The fourth step, post-audit evaluating and reporting of results of investment, is a task that everyone agrees needs doing, but is rarely done. As will be reviewed below, capital investments are projected on an incremental basis, on a cash basis, and on an internal rate of return basis over the life of the investment. Regular financial records and reports are on an annual basis, an accrual basis, or on a rate of return by individual years. A major problem is that many projects become an integral part of a larger, existing investment and the new project cannot be separated from the existing one. The post audit of the incremental segment may become obscure or meaningless. As a result, many incremental investments cannot be appraised against objectives, for example, a large rate of return. The large projected incremental rate of return may become diluted when merged with a larger investment. There may be general disappointment because the new investment results have not lived up to forecasts and, yet, the projected earnings and cash flow of the incremental investment may be right on target. New criteria for post audit may have to be determined to affect post audit for many projects at the time the original projections are made so that management knows how it will measure results against plan. One criterion may be cash flow. Another criterion may be the development of pro forma statements comparing financial income before and after the additional investment, that is, a financial model. The main point is that good budgeting calls for comparisons of projections and results, and though the project evaluation criteria may not be susceptible to audit in many cases, it should not preclude the establishment of other criteria for post-audit purposes at the time the original projection is made. The use of pro forma statements indicating total results as well as impact on earnings per share before and after the investment may be the appropriate basis for appraisal of the additional investment.

Principles of Capital Investment Analysis

This section describes the specific concepts used to evaluate major capital expenditure projects and programs within the scope of the capital budgeting process. The underlying concepts and methods used are examined to bring into focus the economic consequences of a capital expenditure.

When a capital expenditure is proposed, the project must be evaluated and the economic consequences of the commitment of funds determined before referring it to a budget committee for review or to management for approval. How are the economic consequences described best? This is done in two steps:

First, set up the project into a standard economic model that can be used for all projects no matter how dissimilar to each other they may be.

Benefits − costs = cash flow

To describe the formula in accounting terminology:

Benefits: Projected cash revenue from sales and other sources

Costs:	Nonrecurring cash outlays for assets, plus recurring operating expenses
Cash flow:	Net income after taxes plus non-cash charges for such items as depreciation

Thus, if the model were stated in a conventional accounting form it would appear as:

Add:	Cash revenues projected (benefits)
Less:	Cash investment outlay and cash expenses (costs)
Total:	Cash flow

The "benefits less costs" model is usually developed within the framework of the firm's chart of accounts and supported with prescribed supplementary schedules that show the basis of the projection.

It should be apparent that in setting up an economic model, the conventional accrual accounting concept, net income after taxes, has been abandoned. The established criterion is cash flow—net income after tax plus non-cash charges.

Second, adjust the cash flow into relevant financial terms. The cash flow projected for each year over the life of the proposal has to be translated into financial terms that are valid; that is, translate the annual dollar cash flows to a common dollar value in a base year. This concept must not be confused with attempts to adjust for changes in the purchasing power of the dollar.

The calculations assume no significant erosion in the purchasing power of the dollar. Should this occur the time-adjusted common dollar concept may require adjustments for the diminished real value (purchasing power) of future dollar payments. The common dollar value concept used in capital budgeting adjusts for time value only. This is achieved through the development of the concept of discounting and present value that will be examined in the next section. An examination of how a simple two-step model is developed will illustrate the rationale of this approach.

In the first step we set up the economic model: benefits minus costs equals cash flow. To complete this model we need to identify in detail all economic benefits and costs associated with the project. Benefits typically take the form of sales revenues and other income. Costs normally include nonrecurring outlays for fixed assets, investments in working capital, and recurring outlays for payrolls, materials, expenses, etc.

For each element of benefits and costs that the project involves we forecast the amount of change for each year. How far ahead do we forecast? For as long as the expenditure decision will continue to have effects; that is, for as long as they generate costs and significant benefits. Forecasts are made for each year of the project's life; we call the year of decision "Year Zero," the next year "Year One," and so on. When the decision's effects extend so far into the future that estimates are very conjectural the model stops forecasting at a "planning horizon" (10 to 15 years), far enough in the future to establish clearly whether the basis for the decision is a correct one.

We apply a single economic concept in forecasting costs: opportunity cost. The opportunity cost of a resource (asset) is what the company loses from not using it in an alternative way or exchanging it for another asset. For example, if cash has earning power of 15 percent after taxes we speak of the cash as having an opportunity cost of 15 percent. Whenever an asset is acquired for a cash payment, the opportunity cost is, of course, the cash given up to acquire it. It is harder to establish the opportunity cost of committing assets already owned or controlled. If owned land committed to a project would otherwise be sold, the opportunity cost is the after-tax proceeds from the sale. The opportunity cost of using productive equipment, transportation vehicles, or plant facilities is the incremental profit lost because these resources are unavailable for other purposes. If the alternative to using owned facilities is idleness, the opportunity cost is zero. Although opportunity costs are difficult to identify and measure, they must be considered if we are to describe the economic consequences of a decision as accurately as possible. An understanding of this concept of opportunity cost is probably the most critical to this economic analysis and is generally quite foreign to the manager.

At the end of the first step we have an economic model for the project's life showing forecast cash flows for each year. In the second step we convert the results into financial terms that are meaningful for decision making. We must take into account the one measurable financial effect of an investment decision left out in step 1: time. Dollars shown in different years of the model cannot be compared since time makes them of dissimilar value. We clearly recognize that if we have an opportunity to invest funds and earn 15 percent a year and we have a choice of receiving $1,000 today or a year from now we will take the $1,000 today, so that it can be invested and earn $150. On this basis $1,000 available a year from now is worth less than $1,000 today. It is this adjustment for time that is required to make cash flows in different years comparable; that is, discounting.

This time value of funds available for investment is known as the opportunity cost of capital. This should not be confused with the cost of raising capital—debt or equity—or with the company's average earnings rate. Like the opportunity cost of any resource, the opportunity cost of capital is what it will cost the company to use capital for an investment project in terms of what this capital could earn elsewhere.

The opportunity cost of capital is alternatively referred to as the minimum acceptable rate of interest, the marginal rate of interest, the minimum rate of return, the marginal rate of return, and the cost of capital. Whatever the term used, and they are used loosely and interchangeably, it reflects the rate the corporation decides it can be reasonably sure of getting by using the money in another way. It is developed through the joint efforts of management, who identifies relevant opportunities, and the controller, who translates management's judgment into a marginal rate.

Another simple economic concept must be introduced: incremental cost, sometimes called differential cost or marginal cost. By definition, it is the change in cost (or revenue) that results from a decision to expand or contract an operation. It is the difference in total cost. In performing the capital budgeting analysis we deal with incremental costs (revenues) only. Sunk or existing costs are not relevant to the evaluation and decision.

Throughout this study all references to costs and revenues are on an incremental basis.

Rationale of Discounting and Present Value

Discounting is a technique used to find the value today or "present value" of money paid or received in the future. This value is found from the following formula:

$$\text{Future dollar amount} \times \text{discount factor} = \text{present value}$$

The discount factor depends on the opportunity cost of capital expressed as an interest rate and a time period. Table 1 illustrates how discount factors are usually displayed. The discount factors are grouped according to the annual interest rate, expressed as the present value of $1.00, and then listed according to the year the amount comes due. The table should be read this way: When a dollar earns 10 percent per year uniformly over time, a dollar received at the end of the second year is equivalent to (worth) about 86 cents today.

Table 1. Present value of $1.00 at 10 percent.

YEAR	PRESENT VALUE (TODAY'S VALUE)
0–1	$0.9516
1–2	0.8611
2–3	0.7791
3–4	0.7050
4–5	0.6379

Arithmetic and Concept of Present Value

To adjust the model's results for the time element we "discount" both the positive and negative cash flow forecasts for each period at the company's marginal rate of return to determine their present value. This discounting process makes the forecasts equivalent in time. We can now add the present values of these cash flow forecasts to derive the net present value (NPV). The NPV is a meaningful measure of the economic consequences of an investment decision since it measures all benefits and all costs, including the opportunity cost of capital.

When the net present value of a proposed investment is determined we are ready to decide whether it should be accepted. This is done by comparing it to the economic consequences of doing nothing or of accepting an alternative. The general rule followed in comparing alternative projects is to choose the course of action that results in the highest net present value.

Table 2 illustrates the cash flow forecasts and time-value calculations for a typical proposal to invest in a new project when the alternative is to do nothing; that is, maintain liquidity rather than invest. A discount rate of 10 percent is assumed as the company's marginal rate.

The proposed project will cost $500 in year 0, and cash operating expenses thereafter will be $200 per year for four years. Assume the cash benefits will be positive but decline over the four years and total $1,450. The cash flow is negative in the year of investment but positive in the succeeding years and there is a net positive cash flow over the life of the project of $150 before discounting. When the cash flow forecasts are made equivalent in time by multiplying each annual cash flow by the present value of the dollar for each period, the time-adjusted cash flow is determined, and the net present value is found to be $60. The proposed investment is better than doing nothing since all costs are covered, the 10 percent opportunity cost of the corporation's

Table 2. Arithmetic of determining net present value.

YEAR	BENEFITS	COSTS	CASH FLOW	PV OF $1 @ 10%	DISCOUNTED CASH FLOW
0	$ 0	$(500)	$(500)	1.000	$(500)
0–1	425	(200)	225	.952	214
1–2	425	(200)	225	.861	194
2–3	350	(200)	150	.779	117
3–4	250	(200)	50	.705	35
Total	$1,450	$(1,300)	$150		$60 NPV

funds is realized, and in addition, the project will yield an additional $60 return.

Table 2 indicates an NPV of $60. Depending on the cash flow and/or the discount rate, the NPV could be negative or zero. If the NPV were zero, the company would have projected earnings exactly equal to its marginal rate of 10 percent. If there were no alternative projects, and the only alternative were to do nothing, the project with the NPV of zero would be accepted since the company would earn its marginal rate of return. (As explained later, the NPV of zero would yield the discounted cash flow rate of return; that is, 10 percent.) If the NPV were negative because of an inadequate cash flow, assuming the same 10 percent marginal rate required by management, it would mean the project would earn less than 10 percent, and it would be rejected.

There are a number of evaluation methods that are employed in capital budgeting; however, after critical examination of all methods only the arithmetic developed in this simple model will be used to examine three methods used in evaluating capital budget proposals: (1) cash payback, (2) net present value, (3) discounted cash flow (DCF) rate of return—sometimes referred to as the "internal rate of return."

Cash payback is commonly used by businessmen evaluating investment opportunities, but it does not measure rate of return. It measures only the length of time it takes to recover the cash outlay for the investment. It indicates cash at risk. In our model there are costs of $500 committed in year 0. To determine payback we merely add the unadjusted cash flow for each year and determine how many years it takes to get the outlay back. In the first two years $450 is recovered, and by the end of the third year $600 is recovered. By interpolation we find cash recovery to be approximately 2.3 years. It is obvious that the rational businessman does not commit a large sum of money just to recover it. He expects a rate of return commensurate with the risks and his alternative use of his funds in alternative investments (opportunity cost). In our example the calculation of payback reveals a relatively short exposure of funds and cash flow continuing beyond the payback period. It is interesting information in overall project evaluation, but not conclusive. Our model will automatically throw off payback as a byproduct as we calculate the crucial time-adjusted net present value of the investment and DCF rate of return.

A version of cash payback that has come on the scene recently to aid in the evaluation of ultra-high-risk investments is described as the cash bailout method. This approach takes into account not only the annual cash flow as shown in Table 2, but also the estimated liquidation value of the assets at the end of each year. If the liquidation value of a highly specialized project is zero, then cash payback and cash bailout are the same. But if it is assumed in our example that the liquidation value of the investment at the end of year 1 will be \$275, the cash bailout would be one year (cash flow \$225 plus liquidation value \$275 = \$500 original cash commitment).

We consider net present value as described a valid basis for determining the economic consequence of an investment decision. Many business economists use it as their sole criterion for the go, no-go decision for investment. We recognize this method as paramount throughout our analysis but prefer using it in conjunction with other measures rather than as the sole criterion.

Arithmetic and Concept of Discounted Cash Flow Rate of Return

We are now ready to examine the concept of DCF-ROR. It is completely different from the return on investment (ROI) commonly used by businessmen. The conventional ROI is computed for an accounting period, generally on the accrual book figure; investment is taken at original cost although it is sometimes taken at half original cost; no adjustment is made for time value when looked at in the long run.

We are talking about a very different rate of return on investment: The discounted cash flow rate of return in the interest rate that discounts a project's net cash flow to zero present value. Let us expand Table 2, which shows a \$60 NPV when a discount factor of 10 percent is used, to Table 3, which adds a discount factor of 18 percent and yields a \$0 NPV.

Table 3. Arithmetic of determining DCF rate of return.

YEAR	CASH FLOW	PV OF $1 @ 10%	DISCOUNTED CASH FLOW	PV OF $1 @ 18%	DISCOUNTED CASH FLOW
0	$(500)	1.000	$(500)	1.000	$(500)
0–1	225	.952	214	.915	206
1–2	225	.861	194	.764	172
2–3	150	.779	117	.639	96
3–4	50	.705	35	.533	26
Total	$150		$60 NPV		$0 NPV

The DCF rate of return is 18 percent. By definition the DCF-ROR is the rate of return on the project determined by finding the interest rate at which the sum of the stream of after-tax cash flows, discounted to present worth, equals the cost of the project. Or, stated another way, the rate of return is the maximum constant rate of interest the project could pay on the investment and break even. How was the 18 percent determined? By trial and error.

There are many analysts who use the net present value method exclusively; some use the DCF rate of return; others use the two methods to complement each other. Using NPV, positive or negative dollar values are determined with the cost of capital as the bench mark. Excess dollar PV is evaluated and a judgment is made. The DCF rate of return approach ignores the cost of capital in the calculation and determines what the rate of return is on the total cash flow. The result of this approach on our example is to convert the $60 NPV into a percentage. It works out to 8 percent on top of the 10 percent that had been calculated for the NPV. Many businessmen prefer working with the single figure of 18 percent for evaluating a project against a known cost of capital, instead of describing a project as having an NPV of $60 over the cost of capital. It is our feeling that the two methods complement each other, and under certain circumstances one may give a better picture than the other.

Let us reexamine this special DCF rate of return to see what distinguishes it from the conventional rate of return. It is time-adjusted to base Year Zero, so that all dollars are on a common denominator basis; it is calculated absolutely on a cash flow basis; the investment is a definite time-adjusted value; the rate of return is determined at a single average rate over the total life of the investment. Certain implications of this statement require explanation.

The DCF rate of return is calculated over the full life of the project and the accountant's yearly ROI cannot be used to test the success/failure of the new investment. If the planned life of a project is 10 years, and if it can be segregated from other facets of the operation, the DCF rate of return has meaning only when the full economic life of the project is completed. However, in this case it is possible to monitor results on a year-to-year basis by examining the actual dollar cash flow and comparing it with the projected cash flow. (Observe the assumption that the project is separate and distinct from the rest of the operation.)

The one thing that disturbs businessmen most with the DCF rate of return concept is the underlying mathematical assumption that all cash flows are reinvested immediately and constantly at the same rate as that which yields a net present value of 0. In our example in Table 3, 18 percent was used as the discount factor as a constant. Another case could just as easily have indicated a 35 percent rate of return, with the implicit assumption that the cash flow was reinvested at 35 percent. But if the earning experience indicates a cost of capital of 10 percent, how can we reconcile the assumption that we can continue to earn 35 percent on the incremental flow?

Even though a firm's average earnings reflect a cost of capital of 10 percent, the demands on incremental new investment may well have to be 18 to 35 percent to compensate for investments that fail to realize projected earnings. As long as opportunities are available to invest at an indicated 18 percent or 35 percent, it does not follow automatically that it is inconsistent with the average earnings of 10 percent. However, if it is felt that a projected rate of return of 18 percent, in our example, is a once-in-a-lifetime windfall and no new opportunities can be found to exceed the average 10 percent rate, then we are in trouble with our DCF rate of return concept. The reinvestment rate will not stand up. In this situation we have to combine both net present value and rate of return to explain the situation in this way: the 10 percent rate of return of this project covers the opportunity cost of money and throws off an additional $60 cash flow. If other projects of the same magnitude can be found so that the total cash flow generated can be reinvested at the same rate there would actually be a rate of return on the project of 18 percent (the DCF rate of return). The lack of other good investment opportunities is a constraint on the full earning capacity of the project.

We have examined three methods of evaluating investment opportunities. Cash payback evaluates money at risk. Present value measures the ability to cover the opportunity cost of an investment on a time-adjusted basis of money and indicates by a net present value whether the project under consideration will yield a "profit" or a "loss." The discounted cash flow rate of return is an extension of the net present value concept and translates it into a single rate of return that when compared with the opportunity cost of capital gives a valid basis for evaluation.

Since NPV and DCF-ROR concepts take into account the opportunity cost of capital through the discounting technique, it may be stated as a principle that all projects under consideration where this opportunity cost is covered should be accepted. This proposition is both theoretically and practically sound, but three factors need to be considered: How do you determine the minimum acceptable rate of return (the opportunity cost of capital) to select the proper discounting factor? How can you assume no constraints on the supply of capital so that all worthwhile projects can be accepted? How do you take risk into account when examining indicated results? These questions will be examined in the next three sections.

Minimum Acceptable Rate of Return—Cost of Capital

How do you determine the minimum acceptable rate of return (cost of capital) used in discounting? Again a caution: The cost of capital concept used here is not the same as the cost of borrowing. This is probably the most critical factor in the evaluation process. It is a unique and personal rate to each company. There is no guide to look to in other firms. Two firms looking at a potential investment, say an acquisition, may place two completely different values on it. To Company A, with a minimum required rate of return of 10 percent, the investment could be attractive, while to Company B, with a required rate of return of 25 percent, the investment would be totally unacceptable. The difference is centered in the cost of capital to each firm, its opportunity rate of return—the rate that can be expected on alternative investments having similar risk characteristics. An example of the arithmetic involved in reaching this conclusion can be seen when we modify Table 2 to include both a 10 percent and 25 percent discount factor and assume that both companies A and B are the potential sole bidders for an investment with an asked price of $500 and a net cash flow of $150. (See Table 4.)

The investment is very attractive to Company A but completely unacceptable to Company B—it would realize less than its objective of 25 percent. If Company A were in a position to know the cost of capital of Company B it would know that Company B would not bid at all for

Table 4. Comparison of NPV using 10% and 25% discount factors.

YEAR	CASH FLOW	(A) PV OF $1 @ 10%	DISCOUNTED CASH FLOW	(B) PV OF $1 @ 25%	DISCOUNTED CASH FLOW
0	$(500)	1.000	$(500)	1.000	$(500)
1	225	.952	214	.885	199
2	225	.861	194	.689	155
3	150	.779	117	.537	81
4	50	.705	35	.418	21
Total	$150		$60 NPV		$(44) NPV

this investment. Company A would know that it would be the sole bidder.

If a company has successfully earned 25 percent on the capital employed in the firm, an investment opportunity to be attractive would have to yield at least that rate. The 25 percent represents the cost of capital to that firm and an investment opportunity offering only 15 percent would be rejected. A second firm with a 10 percent cost of capital would find the same 15 percent potential attractive and accept it. Thus the same 15 percent opportunity investment is attractive to one and unattractive to the other. Both firms analyzing the identical situation reach different logical conclusions.

Cost of capital in our analysis is *always* considered to be the combined cost of equity capital and permanent debt. We evaluate economic success/failure of a project without regard to how it is financed. Yet we know that money available for investment is basically derived from two sources: debt with its built-in tax saving so that its cost is half the market price for money (assuming a 50 percent tax rate), and equity, which has as its cost the opportunity cost of capital of the owners.

It is necessary at times to break down the combined cost of capital into its components of cost of debt capital and cost of equity capital to put it in terms understandable to the businessman who commonly measures results in terms of return on equity. To illustrate this cost of capital concept, we will assume that a corporation is owned by a single individual whose investment objectives are clearly defined. The total capitalization of the firm is $100, made up of $30 permanent debt capital and $70 owner's equity capital. If preferred stock was outstanding at a fixed cost it would be treated the same as debt. The after-tax

Table 5. After-tax dollar income on investment of $100.

INCOME ON TOTAL INVESTMENT (BEFORE INTEREST)	$30 DEBT × 2.75% COST OF DEBT CAPITAL	$70 EQUITY INCOME ON OWNER'S EQUITY
$ 8.00	$0.825	$ 7.175
9.00	0.825	8.175
10.00	0.825	9.175
11.00	0.825	10.175
12.00	0.825	11.175

interest rate of the debt money is 2.75 percent. The after-tax dollar return on the combined debt and equity capital of $100 under various operations would appear as shown in Table 5.

Restating these dollars as rates of return on the investment of $100, $30 debt and $70 equity, the percentage return on capital would be as shown in Table 6.

If the company has been earning an average of $10 on the total investment of $100, and the cost of debt is $.825, the earning on owner's equity is $9.175. Stated as a rate of return, the $10 earned on $100 is 10 percent return on the total investment (combined cost of capital), and because of the leverage built into the capital structure with long-term debt, the $9.175 earning on equity yields a return on equity of 13.11 percent (cost of equity capital). When there is a 30 percent debt structure and the average cost of debt is 2.75 percent after taxes we can readily convert return on total investment into return on equity by reading our table. It is quite simple to create similar tables for each company and its debt/equity ratio (e.g., with a 50/50 ratio and debt cost

Table 6. After-tax rate of return on investment of $100.

RATE OF RETURN	COST OF DEBT CAPITAL	RATE OF RETURN ON OWNER'S EQUITY
8%	2.75% ($0.825 ÷ $30)	10.25% ($7.175 ÷ $70)
9%	2.75%	11.68%
10%	2.75%	13.11%
11%	2.75%	14.54%
12%	2.75%	15.96%

of 2.75 percent, a 10 percent return on total investment yields a 17.45 percent return on equity capital). If there is the opportunity to invest the company funds in alternative situations, or reinvest the funds in the business and continue to earn at least 10 percent on the combined debt/equity funds, we would describe this as the opportunity cost of capital. This is the critical rate used in discounting: the discount rate used to determine net present value and the bench mark for comparing discounted cash flow rate of return are based solely on the combined cost of capital. The rate of return to the stockholders can be derived and compared with their opportunity cost; that is, their ability to invest their funds elsewhere and earn at least the same rate.

Having decided that return on combined capital is the appropriate criterion for evaluating investment, it is necessary to follow through with this concept when projecting revenues, expenses, and net benefits. If we are to determine net benefits (cash flow) on combined capital, all charges against that capital must be excluded from the expense projections. If interest were charged in the projection, there would be double charging. This is not a novel method; it is used regularly by investment analysts who often determine income before interest on funded debt and before taxes.

As noted, interest expense on long-term debt is not included in the current expense projection because it is covered in the combined cost of capital computation. The interest on short-term debt may be a direct charge to operations if its cost is not in the invested capital base. If the major financing is handled through equity and long-term debt and the short-term borrowing is negligible, this method is acceptable. However, many companies live off their current borrowings and the short-term debt is actually part of the permanent capital. The true leverage would then be reflected in the return on owner's equity when compared with the return on total investment. Once more, a caution: When this method is used, the interest expense on current debt must be excluded from projected costs.

The capital funds of a company constitute a pool of monies for all projects. A particular borrowing rate for additional capital, at a time when a new project is introduced, becomes part of the pool of funds and it becomes part of the average cost of debt relative to total capital. With the addition of new funds it is the average long-run cost that is significant and not the current borrowing rate. The relevant comparison of the projected rate of return is with the average rate for the pool of funds and not the cost of the incremental funds.

In the case of the individual ownership of a corporation, the historical earnings rate can be determined along these lines and a cost of capital for opportunity cost evaluation can become a valid bench mark. If average earnings rise from $10 to $12 there is a new cost of capital, a new cutoff rate for accepting or rejecting projects. This does not imply constantly changing cutoff rates. Some years will be more profitable than other years, some years the cost of debt may be higher or lower than other years, but the earnings of the company are the average adjusted for trend. There is not much logic in setting a cutoff rate at 25 percent when the average is 10 percent just because there was once an isolated year that had unusually high earnings. Many good projects would be rejected because of an unrealistically high cutoff point. The reference point should be actual accomplishment and reasonable expectations, not wishful thinking.

When the assumption of the individual ownership of a corporation is abandoned in favor of a public corporation with a myriad of stockholders, the cost of capital concept gets into difficulty. It is difficult enough postulating the opportunity cost of capital for even a small family, but when we try to postulate the investment objectives of all the different stockholders in a large corporation things become really complex. One stockholder wants cash dividends; another wants growth and reinvestment of earnings; still another wants fast capital appreciation. The opportunity cost of capital to each owner goes undetermined. We are not going to grapple with the problem of cost of capital for publicly owned corporations here because it is a problem that is extremely complex and can be highly theoretical. It is sufficient to note that some large public corporations have been able to develop a cost of capital for their capital budgeting evaluations with some success. Other public corporations have conceded that they cannot develop a cost of capital for all their stockholders and have resorted to a cutoff rate commensurate with their earnings experience. This latter approach violates the opportunity cost concept for the individual owners, but practical considerations have made it necessary to recognize the opportunity cost of the corporation as a person with only minor reference to the real persons who own the firm.

Constraints on Supply of Capital

How can you assume no constraints on supply of capital for investment? Theoretically, if the earnings of a corporation are great enough, and growing fast enough, there is no limit on the amount of debt and equity available. In good basic economic theory, firms should continue their capital expansion until the marginal cost of capital equals its marginal revenue; or stated simply, it is worth borrowing as long as the earnings exceed the cost by even a small amount. The principal limit on debt to the successful corporation becomes the ability of the management to live with it—at what point do the managers start losing sleep because they are so heavily leveraged? However, there are other practical constraints. General business conditions and the state of optimism/pessimism may lead to a limit on the amount of capital a management is willing to commit. There are constraints on the amount of risk a management may be willing to assume; there may be limits on the ability of an organization to handle certain ventures. There are probably other constraints, real and imaginary. In the budgeting process all categories of investments must be classified and weighed. The degree of risk willing to be assumed, and a commensurate return, is something that exists only in the mind of individual managements.

There is no nice formula that can set this. Depending on the management's philosophy, and assuming constraints on availability of capital, the selection may result in the rejection of good safe investments promising a 10 percent return, and acceptance of promotional investments with a great risk promising a 60 percent return, and vice versa. Another constraint mentioned is organization, which may be the decisive factor in choosing between an investment that will make few demands on management and one that will make great demands on management. The latter may offer a superior projected return, yet it may be rejected, reluctantly, because management does not have confidence in its ability to cope with it even though the indicated economic rewards are greater. The practical problems of project selections are varied and complex. While the techniques discussed are hardly the *sine qua non,* they do lend objectivity and direction.

Describing Risk and Uncertainty

How do you account for risk in evaluating the net present value or DCF rate of return? A more accurate term is uncertainty, but risk and uncertainty tend to be used interchangeably by businessmen. The technical difference between the two terms is found in the ability to determine probability of future outcome. Risk, with respect to outcome, implies that future events can be determined within a range of known probabilities, while uncertainty implies that probabilities of outcome cannot be established. Not all proposals have exactly the same element of risk. One investment risk category, the outlay of funds to introduce labor-saving equipment, can be evaluated quite accurately; the projected benefits may be almost a certainty.

Management could even decide to accept all such proposals where indicated NPV exceeds the combined cost of capital. Another category of risk may be the introduction of new product lines. The difference in uncertainty between the two categories is obvious. There probably would be no blanket acceptance of proposals for new products at the cost of capital cutoff rate.

The discount factor remains constant no matter what the risk. The recognition of the different risk categories results in a subjective evaluation of the uncertainties of the venture and a markup on the cost of capital for the go, no-go decision. For example, with a cost of capital of 10 percent, a proposal is made to invest in replacement equipment. There is a modest NPV, little uncertainty. All such proposals would be segregated and acted upon and probably accepted. The second situation, introducing a completely new line or lines whose success is highly uncertain and producing a modest positive NPV, would hardly be acceptable. All such risky proposals would be segregated and judged individually within this special group. To compensate for the uncertainty, a minimum acceptable cutoff rate may be two or three times the cost of capital rate. Average success/failure may actually fall to the 10 percent average cost of capital to the firm.

The determination of the projected rate of return on an investment from the NPV can be arrived at by raising the discount rate until the NPV is zero. This is the DCF rate of return, which is the projected average return on the investment. If such a rate came to 18 percent against a cost of capital of 10 percent, it is still left to the judgment of management whether the additional 8 percent rate of return is adequate to cover the uncertainty of success/failure. This is how risk is usually evaluated—purely subjectively.

There are more exact and sophisticated methods that we will describe. Risk implies probabilities of success/failure. The fact that the project evaluation method we describe here is quite precise and yields a definite answer must not blind us to the reality that decisions are always made in the face of uncertainty. The rate of return description of a project's economic consequences is a single, uncertain prediction of projected revenues and expenses. We cannot ever completely remove this uncertainty. The best we can do is to describe the probable range and intensity of uncertainty involved and the economic consequences of forecasting errors. Next, we briefly discuss three methods that have been found helpful in performing this work.

Sensitivity Analysis

Sensitivity analysis seeks to determine how much a project's net present value or DCF rate of return will be affected (its "sensitivity") when a single factor, or specific group of factors, changes by a given amount. Let's say that for a given project we have been able to predict the volume of product sales with relative certainty, but the price forecast remains very doubtful. To make a sensitivity analysis we would repeat the evaluation using different prices; this would show how much the NPV changes with each price change.

When used with discretion, the results of sensitivity analyses are helpful in estimating the economic consequences of specific forecasting errors. As a minimum requirement, each project evaluation should describe the effect of a wrong forecast in the factor or factors judged most uncertain. However, with analysis of this type we are measuring the effect of change of a single factor or group of factors while all other factors in the projection are held constant. When other components of the projection change, and they are ignored, the new answers may have serious limitations. For example, to change projected prices but to hold volume and costs constant may be unrealistic. We become "practical" at this point and settle for simple sensitivity analysis and get rough answers because manually reworking the model to reflect all possible changes in the figures to determine new cash flows becomes an almost impossible task. In this area computer programs really become significant. Hundreds of single factors can be tested against all other factors and the arithmetic can be worked accurately in minutes instead of in weeks.

Probability Adjustment

Probability is the preferred method of organizing estimates of both the range and intensity of uncertainty for the decisionmaker. In using this method the decisionmaker computes a reasonable range of possible outcomes for the economic model from very unfavorable to very favorable. From them, it is possible to estimate the probability that each will occur. If the unfavorable outcome seems more than the favorable one the project is probably unwise, and vice versa.

An example of probability analysis after the initial projection has been made can be prepared as a test of its validity. No one can forecast with complete confidence and certainty the annual cash flows resulting from projected volume, prices, or even costs. The probability of achievement can be examined by preparing a table of possible deviations from the forecast. Assuming the initial annual cash flows had been projected at $10,000, a reappraisal by management might indicate the following possible results:

5 chances in 100 annual cash flow will be	$14,000
25 chances in 100 annual cash flow will be	12,000
45 chances in 100 annual cash flow will be	10,000
20 chances in 100 annual cash flow will be	8,000
5 chances in 100 annual cash flow will be	0

It is apparent that the projected $10,000 annual cash flow has been reassessed as being the most probable, and there is also an indication of a 30 percent chance that it will be exceeded. However, there is a 20 percent chance that it will be less, and a 5 percent chance that it will fail completely.

There is no precise formula for testing the validity of the judgments that lead to predictions of chances of success/failure. They are based upon subjective judgments of experienced and responsible executives. If this type of analysis does nothing more than force an orderly reappraisal of a project it will serve its purpose. In this example, the conclusion may be that the $10,000 annual cash flow forecast looks reasonable and the initial projection would be allowed to stand. If on the other hand the probabilities of achieving less than the $10,000 had been greater, it would probably lead to a write-down of the cash flows.

The introduction of probability analysis also opens the way to very sophisticated statistical analysis of projected results. Computer programs have been developed that measure probabilities of success/failure of the principal factors making up the projection (volume, prices, costs, etc.), and it is possible to determine projected results taking into account any combination of favorable and unfavorable events. The DCF rate of return is then stated as rates over a range of probabilities. This approach may be extremely beneficial in evaluating major projects, but one must bear in mind that the mathematics is still based on human judgments of chances of success/failure.

Decision Tree Analysis

Some large projects present a wide variety of alternatives with varying degrees of uncertainty. In such cases it may be helpful to clarify the choices, risks, cash flows, and information needs involved by developing a decision tree analysis. This analysis does not require any new measurements. The physical act of preparing a decision tree can, however, force the recognition of alternatives and possible ramifi-

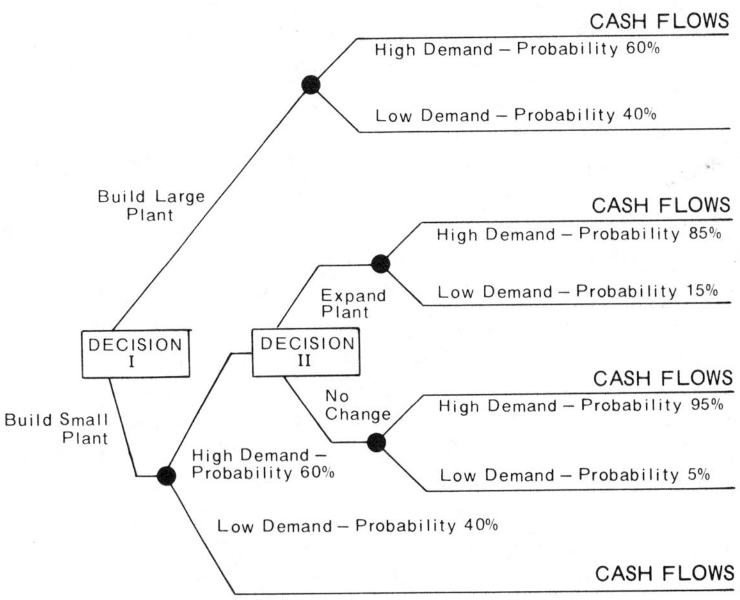

cations of a decision that otherwise might not be seen. A simple decision tree is shown above.

The choice confronting the project sponsor in this analysis is to build a small plant or a large plant. He must evaluate the probabilities of high demand or low demand and the consequences of each with the alternative plants. If a small plant is built and volume develops, a second decision becomes critical: expand or don't expand. The evaluation of these alternatives and the calculation of their economic consequences is facilitated when constructed along these lines.

Project Evaluation

Evaluating components of an investment program for a firm is complex at any time. There are many categories of investments: (a) revenue-producing projects, (b) supporting facilities projects, (c) supporting services projects, (d) cost-savings projects, and (e) last but hardly least, in this era of air and water pollution control, investment required by public authority that will yield no return. Each must be evaluated to determine its incremental consequence.

When a project is isolated from the rest of the operation, evaluation is relatively clear. But sometimes a planned major investment embraces several auxiliary projects which, evaluated by themselves, are not very meaningful. When this occurs, it is necessary to construct a master model that includes all of the projects. Some of the auxiliary projects may not come into being for several years after the main investment is made, and may or may not produce a new positive cash flow. The master model in simple form may take on the appearance shown in Table 7 if individual projects of the types (a), (b), (c) above are assumed (the figures do not add up—only format is demonstrated).

If the three projects are interrelated they should be projected as a single entity. In our example, (a) is assumed to be a major facility that to be successful needs (b) added in three years as supporting facilities; (b) would have no basis for existence if (a) were not created. Project (c) may possibly be identified as a new computer/information system that will produce only costs, but would not exist if (a) and (b) were not created. All costs and all benefits for all corollary investments need to be projected as far into the future as possible to get a true evaluation. Investment evaluations that are made of a project with all the certainty of a DCF percentage can be grossly misleading if the supporting investment of satellites is not taken into account. Actually, these are not separate investments. There is only one—(Project abc). The evaluation has to be of the new single entity. The post audit can be of only the conglomerate single entity (abc).

Projects of the cost-savings category (d) are generally easiest to identify and evaluate. There are relatively clear-cut choices: Invest $40,000 today for new labor-saving machines that will reduce labor costs $12,000 per year; the machines will last eight years, and quality of performance will be unchanged. Determine the NPV and/or DCF rate of return and accept/reject. Such investment opportunities constantly arise, but it is almost impossible to project them as part of a master project. As a result, such investments are evaluated as isolated investment opportunities that may occur in three years, or eight years, or

Table 7. Master project.

PROJECT	NPV	0	1	2	3	4	5	- - -	15
(a)	100	(30)	(2)	14	14	13	13		40
(b)	40	—	—	(15)	5	5	5		20
(c)	(26)	—	(2)	(2)	(4)	(4)	(4)		(10)
Total	114	(30)	(4)	(3)	15	14	14		(50)

never. When they occur, if of major proportions, they affect the potential return on the total investment.

A cost-incurring project (e), such as spend $100,000 to prevent air pollution or be closed up, is one of the few black-and-white decisions a manager faces. Ideally it would be expensed. It may have to be capitalized and written off, and in addition have annual related operating expenses. This nondiscretionary investment falls into the same general category as type (c), support project. The cash flow is always negative and must be included as an integral part of the master investment. If the commitment is large enough it may sharply reduce the original projection and a revision may be necessary.

Selecting Among Projects

On the basis of the techniques for evaluating planned capital investment, it is now possible to move to the methods of selecting among projects. As noted above, in theory, selecting among projects is easy. Invest in anything that when discounted at the appropriate marginal rate will yield a positive NPV. Practically, for many reasons, there are constraints on capital in the minds of most managers. Let us look at the project selection problems that are involved for projects under consideration in a particular risk category when there is a limit on capital.

We have selected the NPV method as the best approach to analyze proposed projects of varying lives. Comparing projects under the DCF-ROR method can be misleading because of the different life factor and the reinvestment factor inherent in each ROR. Excess NPV avoids this difficulty. When the various projects are converted into a profitability index, selection is further facilitated. The profitability index is the ratio of the NPV to investment. For example:

$$\frac{\text{Present value of expected benefits}}{\text{Investment}} = \frac{\$132{,}000}{\$100{,}000} = 1.32$$

In selecting projects when a limit is imposed upon the amount available for investment, we look for the combination that will maximize combined net present value without exceeding the imposed limit. We know that we have reached this goal when we can no longer increase the combined net present value by substituting one project for another and still satisfy the constraint.

A way to achieve a satisfactory combination of projects is through trial and error. As a guide we can use the profitability index (see Table

Table 8. Profitability index.

	NET PRESENT VALUE		INVESTMENT: CASH OUTLAY		PROFIT-ABILITY INDEX
Project A	$1,000	÷	$600	=	1.67
Project B	700	÷	500	=	1.40
Project C	500	÷	400	=	1.25

8). However, such ratios are not foolproof. This is illustrated where there are three possible projects requiring a total of $1,500 in initial outlays, but where $1,000 is the imposed limit.

The choice is between investment in A + C (cash outlay $1,000) or investment in B + C (cash outlay $900). Since A + C have a combined greater NPV than B + C ($1,500 vs. $1,200), A + C should be selected even though C's ratio (1.25) is less than B's ratio (1.40). Such differences are common. The profitability index must always be used judiciously. When there are numerous projects to choose among, the combining process becomes more difficult.

Summary

After examining working concepts of what is involved in the capital budgeting process, the reader can appreciate the many problems that must be resolved when attempting to be "objective" and "scientific" in his capital commitments. The first step is planning the new investment. This is critical. Investments with long life expectancy are wrapped in a shroud of uncertainty, yet plans and projections based on intuition and a minimum of facts are often made with an aplomb that gives the impression of certainty. Hard conclusions and decisions are often reached on the basis of very soft facts. The recognition of uncertainty and its proper evaluation is probably the most important step in the analysis of an investment. Yet this is the area where we often become "practical" because the task is so difficult both in gathering the necessary data and in evaluating them. If all the sophisticated measures of evaluating uncertainty are attempted manually, the paperwork literally becomes overwhelming and it becomes advisable to turn to computer programs for help with the mathematics.

The use of the computer is becoming accepted practice in the capital budgeting procedure. The description of the manual methods of computation already described, and those that follow in the model, assume an aura of certainty. Every attempt is made to approximate the greatest probability of certainty, yet the calculations that evolve from a single measure must be evaluated in the light of uncertainty. The computer programs based upon sensitivity analysis, decision tree analysis, and probability analysis that have been mentioned can now extend our computational abilities.

A program based on a technique known as "Monte Carlo Simulation" makes possible the "simulation" of future events by sampling values from our estimates under favorable and unfavorable circumstances and making all necessary cash flow calculations by random chance. This is an important step forward in the sophisticated handling of uncertainty on the basis of the principles we have very briefly examined. Suffice it to state at this juncture that where computational speed and accuracy are beneficial, computer programs based upon sound theory and principles exist or are being developed. Our primer has recited the principles on which programs have been developed and can be employed advantageously in many situations.

After the development of a plan on an incremental basis, we spent a good deal of time developing and examining recommended criteria for evaluating projected investments. A simple two-step model was developed. The first step, with three elements, is applicable in all situations:

$$\text{Benefits less costs} = \text{cash flow}$$

This is the basis for preparing all projections. The next step is to adjust the cash flow to eliminate time differences. All cash flows are adjusted to Year Zero, which becomes the common denominator for evaluations. The adjustment is made by discounting future values to present values. The mechanics of discounting are not difficult to master but the determination of a discount factor is. The discount factor is the interest rate that equates with the firm's combined cost of capital. This is a relatively new concept and should not be confused with the traditional cost of borrowing. Cost of capital is the rate earned on the combined capital of equity holders plus the permanent debt used as part of the capital of the firm. This simple explanation stands up for the firm with a sole owner who can evaluate the rate of return with his own opportunity cost of capital. When a public corporation becomes involved, the calculation of equity cost of capital could become extremely complex if an attempt were made to take into account the opportunity costs of the various stockholders. For our examination we have simplified the problem by recognizing a combined cost of capital where opportunity costs can be determined. This rate becomes the discount value and is used for discounting.

When proposed investment benefits are discounted at a rate consistent with cost of capital, we have a net present value that tells us that the project will yield more or less than the cost of capital. This rate becomes our cutoff rate when considering accept/reject. Many analysts use this NPV as the sole criterion for evaluation of the project. We recognize the importance of NPV but carry it a step further to discounted cash flow rate of return (DCF-ROR) because the latter changes the excess NPV dollars to a single percentage rate of return that is often easier to comprehend. These two measuring devices that are time-adjusted through the discounting methodology are teamed up with several other criteria to bring the maximum information to bear on the analysis. The most prominent of these is cash payback, which is introduced to reflect money at risk only, and not a rate of return. All these calculations were built on judgments by responsible executives. The final calculations are presented to a budget committee for its appraisal of the facts. The validity of the mathematics used in the projection and final evaluation are dependent on the skill, objectivity, and integrity of the people making the multitude of subjective judgments that are needed at many stages in the development of the projection.

When an NPV or DCF-ROR is determined for a project, and if the company's alternative to investment is to do nothing, the choice is clear. When the choice of capital commitment is among several projects and there is a limit on the amount of capital available for investment, we have chosen to compare projects using NPV rather than DCF-ROR. We are not committed to saying NPV is better than DCF-ROR in all situations, or vice versa. Each has features that work better in some situations.

We recognize the need to control authorized cash expenditures once a commitment is made. Projections of NPV or rate of return are made. If cash expenditures exceed estimates the projected benefits are meaningless. Practically, this has been a pitfall for many good capital budgeting procedures. If large overexpenditures are made, a new projection should be prepared; however, this only yields a new rate of return after the fact. By that time we are merely generating statistics.

Post audit of investment is difficult. It is often neglected. If a plan of post audit is not determined and agreed upon at the time a commitment is to be made, the probabilities are there won't be one or a post audit will be attempted and it may not be satisfactory. As all investments are projected on an incremental basis, and the results are usually part of a larger investment, there is an inability to sort out the results of the incremental portion and identify its NPV or DCF-ROR. It is not fair to management, and it is poor budgeting procedure, to establish a value upon which important decisions are made and then announce you cannot compare the results with the budget. NPV and DCF-ROR indicate expected results over the complete life of the investment, but there is a desire and need to appraise results on an annual basis. For those investments that can be identified apart from other investments, the post audit can be in the form of tests of cash flow and adjusted financial statements. When the investment becomes an integral part of existing investments, the incremental portion cannot be identified and plans must be made to post audit on the basis of the new combined investment. This will involve the preparation of a "master" investment projection at the time the incremental investment is planned. A financial model should be prepared, combined cash flows can be computed if desired, post audit can be performed for the master investment. It is important that this step be taken or the failure of post audit is almost a certainty.

Index

accounting rate of return (AROR)
  as profit evaluation tool, 93, 94
  return on investment (ROI) and, 94–95
accounts, key, *see* clients
accounts, non-key, 24
  as information sources, 75
  see also clients
achievement, as motivating factor, 126–127
action partners, 42–43
added value, as premium justification, 18
adjustment, probability, 187–188
advocate partners, 42–43
affiliation, as motivating factor, 126–127
alliances:
  financial manager, 131–132
  functional manager, 132–133
  purchasing manager, 133–134
  strategies for building, 128–129
  top manager, 129–131
  see also partnerships
analysis
  benefit, 31, 34
  contribution, 159
  cost-benefit, 58–59
  decision tree, 188–190
  equipment configuration, 32, 33, 35
  financial, 33, 35
  incremental, 93–94
  needs, 158–159
  net benefit, 34
  problem, 23, 24, 30, 31
  sensitivity, 187
analysts, securities, as information source, 74
annual reports, 75
answers, to sales representatives' questions, 11–13
APACHE database, *see* database(s), APACHE
APDAB systems components (applications experience and database), 116–117
approval, bottom-up, 39–40
assets, 83
  management's allocation of, 38–39
associations, trade, as information source, 74
AT&T, rebranding strategy used by, 160–161
autocrat partners
  exploititive, 144, 145, 146
  paternalistic, 142, 144

balance sheets
  elements of, 83–84
  examples of, 83, 84
  interpretation of, 84–85
  public company, 82
benefit analysis, 31, 34
bottom-line thinking, 23
bottom tier selling, 5
bottom-up approval, 39–40
brand products, as mature products, 158
budgeting, capital, 169–171
bureaucrats, as decisionmaker partner, 142–143
business function profile, *see* profile, business function
business position, as element of sales strategy, 104–105
Business Week, as information source, 75
buyer-seller roles, 1, 9–10, 17

camaraderie, and partnership, 25
capital
  circulation of, 86–88
  rate of return as affecting, 180–184
  supply constraints of, 184–185
  system strategy as affected by, 184–185

capital budgeting process, 169–171
  capital investment analysis and, 171–174
capital-intensive systems strategy
  capital and, 184–185
  capital budgeting process in, 169–171
  capital investment analysis and, 171–174
  discounting in, 174–184
  general summary of, 192–195
  present value in, 174–184
  project evaluation in, 189–191
  project selection for, 191–192
  risk and uncertainty in, 185–189
"cash at risk," 93
cash flow
  circulating capital principal of, 86–88
  discounted, 93, 94, 177–180
  see also capital
checkpoints, as control standard, 54
circulating capital principle, 86–88
  turnover as affecting, 89, 90, 91
clients
  business position of, 104–106
  database, 72–73, 76–79
  decision-making hierarchy of, 36, 37
  as information sources, 76–80
  need sets of, 135–138
  operations profiles of, 63–70
  profit improvement teams, 147–150
climber, as poor decisionmaker partner, 145, 146
collaboration, as alliance-building strategy, 128–129
commitment, 124–125
competition, 2
  imitation by, 13
  systems, 113–114
conserver, as poor decisionmaker partner, 145, 146
consultants, as information source, 74
consultative selling cycle
  databasing in, 41
  implementing in, 41, 43–44
  penetration planning in, 41–42
  preliminary partnering in, 41, 42–43
  proposing in, 41, 43
contribution margin, 91–93
control standards
  checkpoints for, 54
  construction of, 21, 22
  progress reviews for, 54
  time frames as, 54
  see also incremental analysis
cooperative starter survey, 73
cost-benefit analysis, 58–59
cost centers, 48
cost reduction problem-solving, 18
credibility establishment, 48
current assets, 83
current liabilities, 83
customers, *see* clients
custom-tailored solutions, 11

database(s)
  APACHE, *see* database(s), APACHE
  in consultative selling cycle, 41
  customer's customer, 72–73, 76–79
  electronic, 25
  for function profiles, 72–73
  industry, 73–75
  manual, 25, 26
  opportunities, 103–104
  proposal recycling through, 43
  sales, 2
  sources for, 73–75
database(s), APACHE
  defined, 25
  industry-dedicated, 25–26
  marketcentering, 164
  operations-centered, 25, 27
  problem-oriented, 25, 27
  solution insertion in, 27–28
decisionmakers
  evaluation of function's, 64, 70
  partnerships, 141–146
decision tree analysis, 188–190
declining customer sales strategy, 105–106
dedicated markets, 162–168
dedication evaluation, 12
Department of Commerce, as information source, 74
departnering
  divergent objective in, 150–151
  inequality in, 150, 151–152
depreciation, as systems objection, 111
desensitization of product, 22–23
desystemizing, defences against, 114–117
discounted cash flow (DCF)
  net present value as, 94
  profit evaluation by, 93, 94
  rate of return, 117–180
discounting, 174–175
divergent objective, as cause of departnering, 150–151
documentation, financial, 39, 41
dollar values, *see* financial values
Dresser-Wayne, as manufacturer and marketer of control systems, 28–35

education, as alliance-building strategy, 128, 129
80-20 Rule of Sales Management, 3–4, 10–11, 23–24, 65
electronic database, 25
energy-intensive functions, 66
entry proposal, 46–47
equality, as element of negotiation, 134
equipment configuration analysis, 32, 33, 35
equipment-oriented sales, 19–22
equity, 83
executive, as decisionmaker partner, 142, 143
expense, as systems objection, 109–110
expertise, as consultant skill, 19
experts, as information source, 74
exploitive autocrat, as poor decisionmaker partner, 144, 145, 146

factual knowledge, increasing, 20–21
features-versus-benefits conversion, 22–23
financial analysis: present mix, 33, 35
financial documentation, 39, 41
financial improvement, as top management interest, 129–130
financial managers, concerns of, 131–132
financial role, as element in business profile, 64–65
financial values
  assignment of, 28
  description of, 23
  opportunities determined by, 106–107
  problem solving in, 17–18
  in proposals, 48–49
  as tangibles, 5
fixed assets, 83
follow-on proposal, 43
Forbes, as information source, 75
Fortune, as information source, 75
four-act play, as example of top tier penetration, 38–41
friendship, and partnership, 25
functional managers, concerns of, 132–133

gamesman, as decisionmaker partner, 142, 143–144
General Electric, and marketcentered business groups, 162–163
General Foods, as case history in market-centering, 166–167
give-and-take sessions, 20
glad-hander, as poor decisionmaker partner, 145, 146
government, U.S., as information source, 74
government agency strategy, 104
growth customer strategy, 105–106
growth opportunity, in marketcentering, 167–168
growth strategy, 122–123
  as partnering objective, 123–124

"hurdle rate," in DCF method, 94

IBM
  key market organization by, 162
  profit improvement by, 49
implementation, penetration plan, 40–41, 43–44
incomes, as need sets, 135–138
income statements, 82, 85–86
incremental analysis
  accounting rate of return as, 93, 94
  discounted cash flow as, 93, 94
  payback as, 93
  as profit evaluation tool, 93
  see also control standards
incremental investment, 95
incremental profits, 23
industry-by-industry positioning, 161
industry database, for function profile, 72, 73–75
industry-dedicated database, 25–26
  solution insertion in, 27–28
industry-need specialization, 160
influencers, partnership development with, 138, 140–141
information
  partners, 42–43
  sharing, 20
  sources, 74–75
integration, as profit improvement opportunity, 154, 155–156
integrator, as decisionmaker partner, 142, 143
intensiveness, as element in business profile, 64, 66, 70
intermediate-line thinking, 23
internal rate of return (IRR), as discounted cash flow variation, 94
inventory turnover measurement, 98–100
investment, incremental, 95
investment analysis, capital, 171–174

key accounts, *see* clients

labor-intensive functions, 66
learning, shared, 8
lease option, as aiding in depreciation objection, 111
liabilities, 83

Machiavellian, as poor decisionmaker partner, 144, 145
mainstay proposal, 47
management control systems, 28–35
manual database, 25, 26
marketcentering strategy
  benefits of, 163–164
  examples of, 162–163, 165–167
  general discussion of, 162
  guidelines for, 164–167
  two-way growth in, 167–168
market dedication, 162–163
mature product strategy, 158–161
measurability agreement, as element of partnership, 125
meetings, progress, 22
microanalysis, *see* incremental analysis
migration, sales
  general discussion on, 152–154
  integration as, 154, 155–156
  supplementation as, 153, 154–155
  upgrading as, 154, 155
missionary, as poor decisionmaker partner, 144, 145
mixes, business function
  defined, 49–50
  determining, 70–72
  improvement of, 50–51
  optimal, 33–35
  present, 32, 35
  turnover in, 91
  see also systems, profit improvement
money income, as need set, 135–136, 138
motivation
  of consultants, 135–137
  of customers, 137–138
  evaluation, 12

NCR approach, as case history in marketcentering, 165–166
"necessity and sufficiency" rule, 108
negotiation
  alliance-building, 128, 129
  penetration, 134–135
net benefit analysis: optimal mix, 34
net present value (NPV), as discounted cash flow variation, 94
no-sayer partnership, 138, 139–140
not-for-profit organization strategy, 104

objective definition, 104
objective-oriented penetration, 7
off-the-shelf systems, 24
on-plan/off-plan progress reports, 22
operations, as element in business profile, 64, 65–66
operations-centered database, 25, 27
  solution insertion in, 27–28
opportunity proposal, 47
  see also migration, sales
opportunity system, 48
options
  cost-reducing, 71
  discussion of, 70–71
  generalizations of, 71–72
  revenue-adding, 71
oral presentation, of penetration plan, 40

Pareto Principle, 3–4, 10–11, 23–24, 65
P&L (profit and loss) statements, 82
  elements of, 85–86
participation, as element of partnership, 124
partnerships
  action, 42–43
  advocate, 42–43
  alliance building in, 128–134
  attributes for developing, 123–124
  camaraderie in, 25
  in consultative selling cycle, 41, 42–43
  current customer, 121–122
  customer continuity in, 156–157
  decisionmaker, 141–146
  denominators of, 125–126
  departnering of, *see* partnerships, breakup of
  friendship in, 25
  information exchange in, 73
  knowledge in, 24–25
  motivational factors in, 126–127, 135–138
  negotiation in, 134–135
  opportunities, 152–156
  power source negotiation in, 138–141
  profit objectives in, 7–8, 46
  profit teams for, 147–150
  prospective customer, 122–123
  rights of, 149–150
  rules for, 124–125
  see also departnering
paternalistic autocrat, as decisionmaker partner, 142, 144
payback, as profit evaluation tool, 93

penetration plan
  customer definition in, 102–103
  customer oriented, 8–9
  custom-tailoring of, 105–106
  databasing in, 41
  implementation of, 40–41, 43–44
  negotiation in, 134–135
  objective-oriented, 7
  objectives of, 103–104
  opportunities for, 106–107
  planning, 41–42
  preliminary partnering in, 41, 42–43
  presentations, 40
  proposing, 41, 43
  skill requirement for, 36, 38
  steps for, 38–41
personalized power, 127
plan, penetration, *see* penetration plan
play, four-act, as example of top tier penetration, 38–41
portfolio, profit improvement, 100–101
positioning
  industry-by-industry, 161
  statement, 106
power source negotiation, 138–141
preemption, as system's unique advantage, 113–114
presentation, of penetration plan, 40
present value
  arithmetic and concept of, 175–177
  discounting as determining, 174–175
presidential speech transcripts, as information source, 75
price-performance benefits, 2
pricing, of profit systems, 57, 59
priority time table, 7
probability adjustment, 187–188
problem/opportunity summary, 29, 30, 31, 32, 47, 48, 51
problem-oriented database, 25, 27
  solution insertion in, 27–28
problem solving
  analysis, 30, 31, 32, 34
  APACHE database as aiding, 25–35
  consultative, 17–18
  partnerships, 8
  in proposal process, 47, 48
  standardized, 10–11
  see also strategies, profit improvement
product-centered sales, 19–22
product(s)
  desensitization, 22–23
  identification through, 5–6
professionalism, in customer relations, 19, 21–22
profile, business function
  decisionmaker evaluation in, 64, 70
  financial components in, 64–65
  general discussion of, 63–64
  intensiveness of function in, 64, 66, 70
  operations process in, 64, 65–66
profile, target function
  customer sources for, 76–80
  databases for, 72–73
  industry sources for, 73–75
  information management for, 80–81
  public sources for, 75
profit and loss (P&L) statement, 82
  elements of, 85–86
profit improvement
  as contribution analysis, 159
  contribution margin and, 91–93
  incremental, 23
  needs analysis, 158–159
  objective, 7–8
  prescription, 47, 48–50, 51
  proposals, *see* proposals
  strategies, *see* strategies, profit improvement
  systems, *see* systems, profit improvement
  teams, 147–150
progress meetings, 22
progress reports
  as control standard, 54
  on-plan/off-plan, 22
proposals
  balance sheets aiding, 82–85
  for capital-intense systems, *see* capital-intensive systems strategy
  in consultative selling cycle, 41, 43
  as contribution measurement, 104
  criteria for, 46
  dollar value assignment in, 48–49
  entry proposal as, 46–47
  examples of, 52–53, 54–55, 58, 115
  follow-on, 43
  general discussion of, 45–46
  mainstay, 47
  for marketcentering, *see* marketcentering strategy
  for migration, 152–157
  opportunity, 47
  portfolio, 100–101
  pricing of, 57–59
  problem/opportunity definition in, 47, 48, 51
  profit definition in, 47, 48–50, 51
  recycling strategy of, 154
  system definition in 47, 51

psychic income, 135, 136, 138
psychological input, 21
public sources, for database information, 75

questions, of sales representatives, 11–13

rate of return, *see* return on investment (ROI)
"razor and blades" strategy, 110–111
ready-to-install systems, 24
rebranding strategy
  AT&T's use of, 160–161
  changes needed for, 158–160
  general discussion of, 158
recycling strategy, 154
reorganization, as growth opportunity, 123
reports
  annual, 75
  on-plan/off-plan, 22
repute, as element in partnership, 124
return on investment (ROI)
  accounting rate of return (AROR) and, 94–95
  delivery of, 19
  diagnostic techniques for, 97–98
  discounted cash flow and, 177–180
  evaluation by, 94–95, 104
  formula for, 96–97, 112
  internal, 94
  minimal acceptable, 180–184
  opportunities based on, 95–96
  pricing, 57, 59
  sales consultation, 161
  systems selection based on, 112–113
rights, studying, 79–80
rights of partnership, 148–150
risk(s)
  cash at, 93
  departnering caused by, 150, 151–152
  in discounted cash flow, 185–189
  new market development, 3–4
ROI, *see* return on investment (ROI)
roles
  buyer-seller, 1, 9–10
  of consultative seller, 18
  financial, 64–65

sales management rule, 3–4, 10–11, 23–24, 65
securities analysts, as information sources, 74
Securities and Exchange Commission, 75
security, controls as, 22
self-actualization
  evaluation of, 12
  as need set, 136–138
semistandardized solutions, 11
sensitivity analysis, as determining net present value, 187
servicing, as systems objection, 109, 110–111
shared learning, 8
shared profitmaking, 8
socialized power, 127
solutions
  custom-tailored, 11
  dollar value of, 106–107
  operations installation of, 44
  semistandardized, 11
  standardized, 10–11
sources, information, 73–75
specialization, industry-need, 160
speech transcripts, as information source, 75
stable customer strategy, 105–106
standardized solutions, 10–11
  non-key accounts use of, 24
statements, income
  elements of, 85–86
  as information source, 82
strategy(ies), profit improvement
  alliance-building as, 128–129
  business position as affecting, 104–105
  business profiles for, 63–70
  capital-intensive, *see* capital-intensive systems strategy
  custom-tailored, 11
  declining customer, 105–106
  growth, 122–123
  marketcentering, *see* marketcentering strategy
  objective achievement through, 104
  options in, 70–72
  proposals for, *see* proposals
  "razor and blades," 110–111
  rebranding, 158–161
  recycling, 154
  stable customer, 105–106
  systems for, *see* systems, profit improvement
  target profile for, 72–79
  see also solutions
supplementation, as profit opportunity, 153, 154
suppliers, as information source, 74–75
support, as element in partnerships, 126
survey, cooperative starter, 73

systems, profit improvement
  control standards for, 54
  customer advantages in, 113–114
  definition of, 47, 51–57
  depreciation objection to, 109, 111
  desystemizing of, 114–117
  documentation of, 39, 41
  evaluation of, 93–94
  examples of, 108–109
  expense objections to, 109–110
  general discussion of, 107–108
  management control, 28–35
  mixes in, *see* mixes, business function
  objections to, 109–111
  off-the-shelf, 24
  pricing of, 57, 59
  proposing of, 112–113
  protection for, 159
  as salable unit, 18–22
  selection of, 112–113
  strategies for, *see* strategies, profit improvement
  turnover within, 108
  values of, 28

talent
  management of, 10–11
  mix, 12–13
target function profile, *see* profile, target function
teams, profit improvement, 147–150
technology-intensive functions, 70
television, as information source, 75
10-K reports, as information source, 75
time frames as control standard, 54
time management
  commitment to, 12–13
  downtime and, 38, 50, 57
  Pareto Principle for, 10–11
  profit and, 38
  target, 14
time tables
  migration, 153
  priority, 7
trade associations, as information sources, 74
turnover
  inventory, 98–100
  principle, 88–91
  systems component, 108
two-tier selling, 4–5

upgrade, as profit opportunity, 154, 155

values
  added, 18
  customer, 23
  financial, *see* financial values
  premium, 18
  present, 174–177

Wall Street Transcript, as information source, 75
win-win relationships, 1
  client competition and, 21
  negotiations in, 134
  profit improvement in, 8
workability of solutions, 39–40
workflow, of hospital laboratory, 66, 69
work schedule, 21, 22

Xerox Information Systems Group, vertical selling by, 162

yes-sayer partnerships, 138, 139

zealot, as decisionmaker partner, 142, 143